RED ROWANS AND WILD HONEY

RED ROWANS
and WILD
HONEY

Betsy Whyte

CANONGATE

First published in Great Britain in 1990 by
Canongate Publishing Limited, 17 Jeffrey Street, Edinburgh

Reprinted 1990

British Library Cataloguing in Publication Data

Whyte, Betsy
Red rowans and wild honey.
1. Scotland. Central Region. Itinerants: Whyte Betsy
I. Title
305.568
ISBN 0-86241-281-1

Typeset by Hewer Text Composition Services, Edinburgh
Printed and bound in Great Britain by
Billing & Sons Ltd, Hylton Road, Worcester

Editors' Note

It is ten years since the publication of Betsy's account of her days as a traveller child. That book, *The Yellow on the Broom*, was hailed as a minor classic and is still available in paperback. Almost immediately she was being asked to continue her story, for it had ended when she was still a young teenager travelling the byways of Angus and Perthshire with her mother and sister.

In fact Betsy had already begun a sequel—but progress was impeded by a sudden transformation of her lifestyle. The modest housewife and grandmother, eking out a State pension in a council flat in Montrose, found herself a television and radio personality, travelling England as well as Scotland. In addition to recording traditional songs and tales for the School of Scottish Studies, she gave talks to literary and artistic societies. In classrooms and at folk festivals, she mesmerised children and grown-ups alike with old tales of magic and wonder.

She remained somewhat bemused by her status as a minor celebrity and—although she adapted extraordinary well to this new kind of travelling—she was happy to return home among her family. But a traveller home is no haven for a writer: hers was a 'ceilidh hoose', where friends and neighbours dropped in for a 'crack' at any time of the day and night.

A friendly local librarian helped by providing a little room where she could write in peace—until she grew restless for the open air. Then Betsy returned to her more relaxing, if backbreaking occupations such as collecting whelks along the rocky Angus shores or working for farmers during the weeding and harvesting seasons.

Parts of her manuscript appeared intermittently over the next five or six years until—encouraged by a writer's bursary from the Scottish Arts Council—Betsy felt it was nearly finished. She had taken her story up to the end of World War Two, telling with vivid detail and candour of her days of courtship of her mother's struggle to cope with the problems of being a widow and mother of four. Like many other traveller women, she toiled to keep the family together while their menfolk were away fighting Hitler's armies.

But Betsy found great difficulty in rounding off this book. There seemed no natural way to end it, for she already had a sequel in mind which would bring her story up to date. Only parts of the sequel were put down on paper but we were given other fascinating glimpses of what was to follow and tried repeatedly to persuade her to continue without delay.

But—even when *Red Rowans and Wild Honey* was completed to her satisfaction—she remained adamant. 'I have not been writing. It is just a traveller superstition, not to count chickens . . . If a publisher is found then I will write night and day. It is all in my mind. I will only have to set it down.'

Sadly, it was not to be. Three days after she wrote those words, still before she knew that this book would be published, she died of a heart attack.

Over the years we worked with her, we were constantly amazed by the talent—and the humility—of this remarkable woman. She herself recognised only one 'gift': that of second sight, inherited from her mother and to Betsy it was disturbing. But she was indeed a gifted, natural, writer: or rather a storyteller turned writer. All her written material *was* actually composed in her mind. Her laboriously penned sheets bore little trace of amendments and corrections, the signs of a seasoned writer's second thoughts. Read aloud by one familiar with it, her narrative flowed effortlessly without pause: the natural breaks were there—but unsignalled. Formal punctuation, spelling, paragraphing, seemed necessary to help the reader to 'listen' as Betsy intended. But that was all: we call ourselves 'editors' for lack of a better term: in fact we were mainly exhorters, advisers, sounding boards . . .

Constantly she questioned the value of her writing: 'Will

people really want to read about that?' Yet she was not only recording a past way of life and the attitudes it shaped. In writing of her own life with all its joys and sorrows, its 'red rowans and wild honey', she told of life itself in a way no contrived novel can. Because these events really happened, because 'civilised' people really did so behave towards those they regarded as their inferiors . . . her story in singularly poignant, thought-provoking, disturbing . . . Perhaps because, despite the trials and tribulations, the humour and the hope shines through?

Peter Cooke, Ian Gould.

I

'Do you hear me, lassie?'

'Aye, Ma, what is it you're saying?'

'That's three times I have spoken to you and got no answer. There's more for you to be doing than sitting dreaming. Go with Katie along to the stable and yoke the pony. The poor animal will be foundered if it doesn't get out for a run. Anyway, there's nothing for it to eat. You can cut some grass for it.'

There was a note of irritation in Mother's voice. She was worried. My father had died some six weeks earlier, leaving her with three girls. Katie, the eldest, was twenty. I was fifteen, then there was Lexy, eleven.

Mother had been living in a state of confused despair since Father's death, quite unable to put her mind to anything much. At first she had wandered through the house singing coronachs to her aching heart, with tears running down her cheeks. This doleful singing had such a depressing effect on all the rest of us that one day I burst out, 'For God's sake, Ma, stop that or you are going to put an end to all of our days.' She did stop it and tried very hard to keep her heart up.

There was neither bite nor sup in the house, so when I answered Mother it was to say, 'I could do with something to eat myself, as well as the horse. Give me your basket with your wee bits of stock and Katie and I will try to raise the wind.' 'Stock' was what we called whatever we were selling—in this case such things as needles, pins and bootlaces.

Ricky, my little Border collie, had been lying quietly under a chair but he soon stirred himself when he knew that I was going out. There was a pleading look in his brown eyes as he gently pawed me. Kneeling down and fondling him, I told him that he couldn't come with me.

The look in his eyes as I opened the door was heart-rending. So I ran back to him and said, 'I will be back for you in about twenty minutes. You be a good wee doggie and I'll take you with me.'

Then, going over to where Mother was sitting, I put my face up close to hers and said, 'Do you think there is any difference in my freckles? Are they going away?' Mother had told me to try rubbing the freckles with a slice of raw potato every night. I had been doing this for a fortnight now, and I was sure they were fading.

This was too much for Katie, who had been impatiently waiting for me. 'Is that all you can think about?' she said. 'Folk's insides are croaking out of them with hunger and all you can think about is getting rid of freckles!'

'Can you two lassies not look at each other without having an argument? You will both live peaceably in less room yet.' Looking at Mother's pale face, and her eyes without any light in them, made a profound wave of pity almost rend me. She scanned my face too, and I knew that she was not examining my freckles but reading all the secret emotions of my heart. I also knew that she didn't have a smoke and that she could suffer the pangs of hunger but having no tobacco really downed her.

I ran ben the room and took a gold bracelet out of a drawer. I had gotten it from a farmer's daughter up at Glenisla. Coming back to Mother I said, 'Here, Ma. Take that up to the jeweller and he will surely give you the price of tobacco for it—and a bite for us.'

'That's the bracelet that you got from Isla. I couldn't take it and sell it. I know how much you like it.' Mother weighed the heavy eighteen-carat bracelet in her open palm as she spoke. 'You are never likely to get anything so nice as this again, Betsy.'

'I ken, Ma, but the only reason that I am so fond of it is because of the way I got it. It is only a thing and cannot feel the craving for a smoke, nor hunger. I am much too camaschacht to wear it, anyway. It is better for us to get something for it than it is for me to wear it, or to just have it lying in a drawer.'

2

I had picked up Mother's square basket and was going towards the door as I spoke. ''Bye, Ma. Lexy is playing pea-alleys out the back.'

Katie, who had been waiting for me at the gate, gave me a look that would have sunk the *Queen Mary* when I came out. But she said nothing—for a wonder.

Prince the pony nickered when we entered the stable— which was only about three hundred yards from the house. Katie had been handling horses since she was a child but I, for some odd reason, never felt quite at ease with them. Nor did horses seem to be quite at ease with me. My very presence seemed to disturb them in some way. They could tolerate me in the float or cart—and eventually settled down, after a few nervous quivers, if I got on their backs—but it was another story if I approached them face on. Then they would really show their uneasiness.

So I was a bit bothered when Katie said, 'Will you put on the brecham whilst I get the rest of the harness?' She had led Prince out of the loose box.

The brecham was hanging on a nail. I lifted it off and approached the pony. He was a canny, gentle beast but as I neared him he backed a little and showed me the whites of his eyes. I just knew that he would rear if I got any closer to him. 'You had better put the brecham on,' I shouted to Katie.

'All right, bag of laziness. You that wants to do nothing but sit and read, or look down at your own face in the looking-glass all day. I'll put it on myself.'

She was beside me now and picking up the brecham from where I had thrown it down. 'You are as white as a sheet,' she said and began to laugh mockingly. 'I think you are feared of the pony.' Katie knew nothing of this thing between me and horses. 'You who are always the brave one! Oh aye, you are a brave body!'

Her mocking words and laughter were too much for me. I snatched the brecham from her, and boldly approached Prince with it raised towards his head. He nickered, backed and reared—and I had to dodge his hoofs as he came down again.

'See! He is the one that is feared, Carrots, not me.' I called Katie 'Carrots' because she had red hair.

'You must have been doing something to the animal or he wouldn't be like that with you, Peesie.'

Katie called me Peesie ('Peewit') because every spring, when the fields were ploughed ready for potato planting, I would walk up and down the drills collecting peewits' eggs. I would break one and if it was fresh I would take the rest. If they were gogged I easily knew, and just left them. At the same time I felt sorry for the birds but, as the potatoes had to be covered with soil ploughed over them, those eggs would probably have been crushed into the earth anyway. So I thought that we were better to eat them than to have that happen to them. Nice and tasty they were, too.

I have often seen ploughmen, when they were happing the potatoes, being alerted by the frantic screeching of the parent birds. They would stop their horses and search in front of the ploughs for baby birds or gogged eggs. This was no easy task as the peesie builds no nest and just lays her eggs on top of the earth. They are so well camouflaged that you could pass them a dozen times and not see them. However, if a ploughman did find them, he would gently lift the eggs or newly hatched birds and carry them over to where the plough had already been—hoping that the parents would find them.

I think it is about time that I went back to Katie and Prince at the stable. Katie's last remark had stung me. I would never ill-use a dumb animal, but I was reluctant to explain things to her. I was very reluctant to accept the fact that horses disliked me, so I did not want to talk about it.

Katie soon had the horse yoked—with very little help

4

from me. 'Should we go out the Montrose road?' Katie asked.

'There is always a lot of traffic and people walking on that road,' I answered her. 'We could be better going down the Muddy Brae and over the bridge—but stop at the house first. I'm taking Ricky with me.'

Ricky bounded toward me when I entered the house. 'Oh, did you think that I had forgotten about you, my wee jugal? Come on, jump into this box—and not a sound out of you, mind!' I placed an empty cardboard box on the floor as I spoke and he leapt into it. Then I covered him up with an old jacket.

Mother, who was combing and pleating Lexy's long hair, said, 'That animal is wiser than many a human being.' Ricky's intelligence was almost astounding. He seemed to be aware of all that went on around him and most of what was said of him he seemed to understand. We lived in a council house and were not allowed to keep a dog or any other animal. Ricky always hid himself when anyone came into the house.

I carried out the box with Ricky in it and placed it on the float, then Katie and I set off. When we had crossed the old bridge and left the town, I lifted the coat off the top of Ricky. He scrambled out of the box and started to demonstrate his delighted pleasure as only a dog can. He loved sitting on the cart or running alongside and jumping in again when he got tired.

Katie had started the horse to trot and I soon got lost in the beauty of the scenery. This road ran for about three miles along the wooded bank of the river South Esk and mossy green dykes ran along each side of it. A brilliance of wild flowers patterned the grass and couthy masses of honeysuckle caressed some of the trees.

Katie pulled up when we came to a wide verge covered with lush grass. 'I'll bet you never took the huke with you,' she said.

'I can use the scythe,' I told her. Daddy's scythe was fixed under the float where he had made a place for it in case of accident. I could see that even the look of the scythe blade made Katie nervous, so I reassured her saying, 'I've cut with a scythe hundreds of times.' I hadn't really, but I could use it. Father had showed me—after I had insisted. My two brothers had died in childhood, so I tried to be like a son to him, helping him with almost everything he did.

The pony was already sampling the grass and Ricky had found a wandering toad which seemed to interest him a lot. As I grasped the two handles of the scythe I realised that Daddy's hands had been the last to hold them and waves of deep emotions pulsed through me. I sighed deeply.

Then I started to sing *The Boatie Rows*, keeping time with the scythe and with one eye on Ricky—lest he should get tired of the toad's manoeuvres and come bounding into the scythe. Katie had finished the song with me then, jumping up onto the float, started to diddle *Paddy O'Rafferty* and to do an Irish clog dance with her feet rattling on the wooden float. She had learned this from some Irish potato workers who had been living in huts at a farm where we too were working. 'Come on, Katie!' I shouted in an Irish accent.

Just like that the pony decided to move on a bit, to better pastures—jerking the float as it did so and sending Katie sprawling across it. Her laughter assured me that she was unhurt so I too started to laugh and we kept on laughing for some minutes.

'Aye, this is all right and right enough, but it's not filling our bellies any. We'd better hurry up and get on the road.' Katie had begun lifting the cut grass and piling it onto the float as she spoke, keeping well away from where I was using the scythe. 'Could you do with a reeking jug of yellow tea and a pipe packed full of fine black tobacco?' I asked her.

'Shut up, Peesie, or I'll hit you,' she answered. Soon there was enough grass cut so I stopped and secured the scythe back into its place under the float, then helped Katie to lift the grass—just piling it loosely.

Ricky was sitting on top of the grass, panting. 'Poor wee jugal, tired out chasing a yirdy. What like would you be chasing a mootyay?' I crooned to him. He alerted when I mentioned 'rabbit', then tried to lick my face. Ricky knew a lot of words in cant, the secret language of the travelling people. I taught him as many as he should know, for it came in useful sometimes.

Jumping up on the float, we then drove on till we came to a row of cottar houses. Taking turn about, Katie and I went to all the houses—on and off the road for the next five miles—trying to sell something out of Mother's basket. But it was no go. Often people just did not have money, or anything else to spare, in those hard-up thirties.

So Katie turned the horse and we started to jog back along the road. We were a bit tired and very hungry. We were also gasping for a smoke, having acquired the habit at a very early age.

3

Passing an opening in the dyke at the side of the road, I asked Katie to stop. 'I'm going to have a rake in the midden down there,' I told her.

'The middens around here are well enough raked,' she answered.

The midden was a place where surrounding farmers dumped cartloads of rubbish. It was on the steep wooded bank leading down to the river, and much of the rubbish had rolled down, to end up against fallen or upright trees. It was also skirted with waist-high nettles, the most cantankerous nettles I had ever encountered. Already I could feel their venom in my legs. The stench of rotten potatoes and other vegetation nearly knocked me down, but I had seen four stone jam jars amongst them, and was determined to get them. In those days a penny would keep your electricity or your gas going all day, and those stone jars were worth a penny each.

I scrambled up the bank, to tell Katie. 'In the name of God, lassie, what are you doing? Oh me, me, the toich coming off you would gas a regiment of soldiers,' Katie greeted me, holding her nose.

'I just came up to tell you that I've found four jars and I'm going down to the burn to wash them.'

The burn was really the river South Esk. We called all rivers burns—big burns or wee burns, never rivers.

She was backing away from me, still holding her nose and repeating, 'What a toich!'

'You'll no say that there's a toich off the coppers I'll get for them, Carrots.' The pain of the nettle stings was more to blame for my stinging words than Katie's remarks. 'Come on, Ricky. Come away from that bool-nosed woman.'

Ricky readily obeyed and Katie shouted after me, 'Wash yourself too, Peesie, or you needn't come near me!'

I stood up past the knees in the river as I washed the jars, which were half full of glaur and were stinking.

Ricky was all but the tail into a rabbit hole, and seemed to be pulling and dragging something out. So I went to see what it was. 'What's that you've got, Ricky?' I could see that it was a sack. So I helped Ricky pull it out. It was very heavy and when I looked inside, my eyes met another pair of eyes. The dead eyes of a huge salmon. There were five big salmon inside the sack. The fish were quite fresh and must have been caught that morning.

Poachers, I thought. Well, I'm sorry, poachers, but you're going to be one salmon short when you return tonight. If daylight caught out poachers they often hid their catch and returned for it after darkness. Now, how to get the jars and the fish up the slippery bank?

I sat down and took off my stockings, and laced one through the salmon's gill. Then I tied the jars at intervals along the other stocking. The wet stockings tightened and held them quite securely.

I had meant to carry the jars slung around my neck and under my arm, but in my mind I could hear Mother's voice saying, 'Have you no more sense than that, lassie? If you slip and fall, those jam jars could break and pierce you. They could even be the cause of your death.' So I changed my mind and tied the other end of the stocking which was on the salmon to its tail. Then I put my head and one arm through the ring so the fish was resting across my shoulders. You see, I needed a free hand to grasp branches of trees and roots of grass to help me up the slippery brae, and I had to drag the jars behind me with my right hand.

I heard Katie shout, 'Loo-ral!, loo-ral!' and I 'loo-ralled' back to her. I knew that she couldn't leave the pony, and also that she was fed up waiting for me.

Reaching the road I quickly off with the fish and pushed it under the grass on the float. The jars were a bit muddy, but at least they were no longer smelly. They, too, went under the grass.

Katie was a bit stunned at the sight of the salmon. 'Did you catch that?' she asked.

'Dinnae be stupid,' I told her.

Katie was really upset. 'We will be jailed if anyone sees that.' She said no more but her face was rather pale.

It was a warm day and I could feel the mud drying on my face. There was a horse trough at the side of the road about two miles from the town and, after the pony had taken a drink, I tried to clean myself with the water while Katie washed the basket. Katie had a comb in her pocket and I tidied my long hair.

'Give me a shot of your coat,' I asked Katie. 'The worms are eating the insides out of me. I am going down to that farm to ask for something to eat.' Covering my dirty dress with Katie's coat, I made sure all the stock was in the basket.

'I'll take you down,' Katie said, and turned the pony down into the farm road.

4

When we got to the farm the door was opened to me by a dark-haired, rosy-cheeked, sparkling-eyed servant maid. She's as healthy as a trout, I thought.

'It's nae often that we get ony o' you lads up here,' she exclaimed.

'Maun dae is a good master,' I answered.

'If it's siller you're seeking you're gaen tae be disappointed,' she told me. The dried mud on my dress and my tangled hair had let her know at once who I was, or rather what I was.

'The master and missus are away from home,' I stated, rather than asked.

'Aye, they are away tae the mart today.'

'What about these?' I asked her, holding up a box of pretty fancy garters. 'Your lad will love them.'

She blushed crimson exclaiming, 'Foo dae you ken I have a lad, and that the master and missus are away? Ye can read fortunes can't ye? Come on, read my fortune for me.'

'Well, I dinnae really,' I began, then desperation took over. 'I suppose I could,' I told her.

'Haud on a meenit!' she shouted, running into the house, and returned in a few minutes holding out a gold ring set with emeralds and pearls. 'You can hae this ring,' she said.

'Na, nae way will I take your ring,' I told her.

'It winna fit me,' she told me. 'It belonged tae ma Granny.'

'Na, na, I cannae eat a ring, lassie, I dinnae want it.'

'But ye can sell it.' I believe she would have given me the farmhouse on my back, she was so keen to get her fortune told.

'Put that ring away,' I told her, 'and tell me what like a mistress you have?'

'I hae a braw mistress, and master tae. They treat me like I was their ain.'

'Then maybe she wouldn't miss a puckle oatmeal or tatties and such like, and maybe three jam jars.' I was determined to get the price of half an ounce of tobacco for Mother.

So we struck a bargain. My fortune telling delighted her, and she nearly filled a white flour bag which nearly all travelling people—women anyway—carried for this very purpose. 'Now don't give me anything that will be missed,' I told her. At that time most farms kept big chests of tea, sacks of flour and oatmeal, also sugar. They also made their own butter and cheese and hung their own pork from the rafters to smoke. Eggs were plentiful, too, and that young servant girl was more than generous. However, I knew that she spoke the truth when she said that her mistress wouldn't miss any of it.

I bade her goodbye and came away laden with the bag on my back, and Mother's big square basket on my arm.

5

When I rounded the corner of the steading and came to the farm road I saw that a policeman was standing holding his cycle and talking to Katie. Hell, I thought, God pity him! Ricky was nowhere to be seen. I guessed that he would be under the grass on the float: he had been taught to hide from policemen. Anyway, Katie would have hidden him when she saw the policeman approach.

As I neared them Katie glanced my way, then said to the policeman 'OK, there she is now. I told you I was waiting for my sister. There I go saying "OK." We are all picking up that American slang from the talkies.'

The word 'slang' was the one I had been waiting for. In cant it means 'licence'. So I immediately knew that the policeman had been asking Katie if we had a licence. For a moment I almost panicked. We had no licence for peddling. We did not even have a dog's licence for Ricky. Then there was that salmon under the grass. If the policeman discovered it, then we would be in real trouble. I scanned his face, then relaxed a bit. His howlet eyes and sticking-out ears, the general look of his face, had told me that his intelligence was rather limited.

'Well well, then,' he said to me, 'and what have you got in the bag?' The maid had put the eatables into the flour bag for me and I had it on my back with the basket on my arm.

'Just some gather-me-goes,' I answered him lightly.

'What the hell are gather-me-goes?' he asked. 'Let's have a look.'

Laying down the basket, I let the bag slip around my

shoulder—still holding it, of course—and held it open for him.

'What's all this? Tatties, eggs, jam, bread. . . .' His head was almost into the bag and he lifted each article as he mentioned its name. 'You don't intend to be hungry anyway. Is this what you call gather-me-goes?'

'Aye,' I answered him, 'we gather them as we go.'

'Well, let's see your licence now—and don't try to tell me that you've left it at home. I will soon find out where you bide. There is not so much scouff for you lads now since they started to close down the camping sites. I was caught like that once before. One of your menfolk told me that his driving licence was at home where he was biding. I trailed away up to the Cattle Rake the next day, but the cottar folk told me that none of you lads had been there for weeks.'

When he had finished talking, I told him that I didn't need a licence.

'What do you mean, you don't need a licence? Didn't I catch you red-handed, coming away from a door with your basket and everything? You need a pedlar's licence for that.'

'Aye, you saw me coming away from a door but I wasn't peddling. I was swapping, exchanging things for food. If you go and swap a book or anything, do you need a licence to do it? There is no such thing as a licence for swapping. Leastways if there is I've never heard about it.'

At this the policeman pulled a wee book from his pocket, saying, 'I've only your word for that.'

'You have more than my word. You've seen the things in the bag that I've been swapping for. You can search me and Katie and inside the basket, and I can swear that you will not find one farthing. I'm telling you I only swap.'

'Well, well, I'll just have a look through the book and see if it says anything about that,' he said. He began to read his little book laboriously, taking what seemed half an hour to each page.

I was getting a bit irritated now—tense lest Ricky should come out. I could see the grass heaving a little above him. So I lifted the bag and the basket and put them on the float—jumping up onto it myself too. Katie was already sitting on it with the reins in her hand. 'You will have to excuse us, policeman. We have weans coming out of school. You will have no bother finding us as we have a house in Brechin—and have had for years. You yourself must be new to the place or you would know us.'

So saying, I gave him our names and address. Then Katie put stirr to the horse which had been feeding away contentedly at the grass on the verge of the road. The policeman was still standing peering into his wee book when I looked back. His cycle was propped against the paling. He had shouted, 'Hold on a wee,' but we had just kept going. 'That man is pure glaikit,' I told Katie, 'God pity him.' As I spoke, I opened the meal poke and gave Katie one of the fine cheese sandwiches which the maid had made up for me—taking one to myself as well.

I knew that Katie was really hungry, but she still had the sandwich in her hand after I had almost devoured mine with one bite. 'You heartless wee bitch!' she shouted at me. 'You would really stuff your own inside knowing that your mother and wee sister are at home without a bite.'

'Are you mad, you carotty-headed, plukie-faced creature? To think that I would do such a thing! Didn't I give Mother my gold bracelet to sell? She would surely get the price of a bite for herself and the weans for it.'

Katie didn't say another word but rived into the sandwich. There were several more sandwiches and we ate them very quickly.

Just like that who should come alongside us but the constable on his cycle. 'Pull up a minute, you two!' he shouted.

We thought it best to comply. 'What now?' I asked him.

'I just want to have a wee look at this beast,' he answered, going up to the horse's head and examining its teeth, ears and neck.

Now Prince was what Mother called 'ewe-necked' and always ran with his head to one side as if he was going to run into the side of the road. The policeman came round to the side of the float again, saying, 'He seems to be all right.

I thought he had a sore on his neck or something. You're surely pulling your left-hand rein too tight. I was watching him as I cycled along behind you and every minute I thought that you were going to run into the dyke.'

A fat lot he knows about horses, I thought. So I said to him, 'Oh well—you see, policeman, it is like this. We bought him from a man in Kirriemuir and he keeps trying to turn round and go back to him.'

Katie quickly put the horse in motion lest I would say too much, saying 'Shaness, shaness! We really have to hurry, constable, for the sake of the weans,' she shouted back to the policeman.

'You'll get your desserts one of these days for your impudence, Peesie,' she warned me.

Ricky had seen the constable coming up behind us and had burrowed under the grass himself. He was now struggling to emerge again but I said, 'Plank, Ricky! He's coming again.' This time, however, the policeman just cycled past us, giving a little wave of his hand.

'He surely didn't know that you were being impudent or trying to make a fool of him,' Katie said. 'Does he really believe that the horse is trying to turn around?' Then she burst out laughing.

Soon we reached the town and I asked Katie to wait at the door of our house till I got Ricky smuggled in. As I had left the cardboard box in the stable, I had to wrap him into Katie's coat and rush inside with him.

At the stable we hid the big salmon in Mother's square basket, putting the stock on top of it with the newspapers in between.

'You take one side of the handle and I'll take the other,' Katie said—as the basket was now very heavy.

As we walked the short distance home, we saw two other policemen walking towards us. 'Hell to my soul,' Katie said, 'if they don't stop us.' They did.

'Well, girls, and what have you got in the basket?' one of them asked while they barred the way.

Katie's face got red—but with anger. 'We have a big

salmon in the basket,' she said. 'We've been poaching salmon all day.'

They both laughed heartily and moved out of our way.

'If you tell them the truth, they'll not believe you!' Katie was laughing now and I joined her.

6

Mother's first words when we got inside the house were, 'You two have made a day of it, haven't you? I was beginning to think that you had met two young men and run away with them.' She was trying hard to be cheerful.

'I did get a young man and Katie—you know what red-heads are like—she got two. Handsome young policemen, they were.' I too spoke cheerfully.

Mother's eyes scanned me and she laughed in spite of herself. 'It's a wonder that all the young men in the district aren't chasing after you.'

Looking down at myself, I could see the reason for Mother's words. My dress and shoes were caked with mud!

I could see that Mother had gotten food, so I asked her if she had managed to sell the bracelet.

'Aye,' she answered, 'but wait till I tell you about it. I didn't want to trail away up to the top of the town, so I went into that first wee jeweller's up there. He looked at the bracelet and asked me to wait a minute while he tested it in the back shop. He came back in a wee while and started speaking away about this, that and the next thing as if butter wouldn't melt in his mouth. Fine I kent that he had phoned for the hornies. So I asked him if he was going to buy the bracelet or not, and if not to give it back to me because I was in a hurry.

'Says I, "Nae hummin' and hawin', Mister. Just you hand back what belongs to me or I'll have something to tell the police when they do come. You with the yellow jaws, if you kent what was eating at your liver you would be praying for your soul instead of getting the police to me. Just because you would rob your own grandfather," says I, "you think that I would do the same." ' Mother had a habit of saying 'says I' or 'says she' when she talked.

'We've all had a day of it with the police,' Katie said. 'What happened after that, Ma?'

'Well, I was more than an hour standing in that shop. Me and the wean. I was nearly dropping on the floor with weakness, but take what I was giving to that jeweller all the time. When the police did come, as God would have it, one of them was Sergeant Wilson. The jeweller was determined to be heard first. The words came clattering out of his mouth like chuckie stanes on a tin. That's the kind of voice he has. I just stood and said nothing. If you had heard the things that he was telling the police! "Where would anybody give a thing like that away—and especially to they kind of folk?"

'He didn't half get a surprise when Sergeant Wilson turned round to me and, putting the bracelet in my hand, said, "Here's your property, Maggie. You look as if you are going to pass out, so come on outside." '

' "Aye," says I, "I'm no' feeling very great yet." '

'Once outside the shop he put his hand in his pocket and handed me two half-crowns. "Take that and go and get a wee bite for yourself and the bairns," he said. I offered him the bracelet but he wouldn't take it.'

Lexy had been busy making tea while Mother was talking. She had also fried some bread and now she was handing it around to us. 'It's a good job that the policeman knew you, Ma,' she said.

'Bairn, I've known Sergeant Wilson since he was a lump of a laddie. His father was cattleman at the Fornet, a farm where we used to work.'

Lexy was anxious to know about our encounters with the police that day. So Katie told her all about it while I went to clean myself up. Soon I could hear them all laughing.

Mother was in the scullery, sawing the head off the salmon, when I came ben again. 'Ma,' I asked her, 'is it a sin to tell fortunes? I read a servant maid's hand today and I took that jam and things from her.'

'Ach, dinnae worry about that, but never take anything for doing it except when you're really in dire need. There's something uncanny about being able to read fortunes but, as long as you don't sin your soul, I think it should be all right. Your father, God rest him, used to sit watching you for hours when you were a wean. "You had better keep that lassie right, Maggie," he would say to me. "She is a pure fairy. Ower old a head for such wee shoulders." Aye, lassie, it's not an easy thing to carry around with you. Mony a silent tear you'll shed because of it.'

'Oh, Ma, dinnae tell me that,' I said as I watched her scrape the scales off the salmon and plunk its eyes out. She wasn't going to waste the head. 'Well, Ma, I'm awa' to get the jam jars and sell them before the shops shut. I'll give you the money to go to the pictures with.'

This was typical. It never entered our minds to keep the money for another day. To our way of thinking, there might never be another day. And nearly all travellers love any form of entertainment. Many would walk miles to the nearest town and go to the pictures with their last penny. Mostly the men and the young unmarried ones—but Mother was very fond of the pictures and would laugh like a child at the strange behaviour of the people on the screen.

Mother was swithering. She thought it was too soon after Father's death for her to go to a picture hall, but Kate persuaded her. 'There's no harm in doing that, Ma. Come on, I'll go with you.'

7

So off they went, leaving Lexy and me with at least a dozen warnings to take care of ourselves.

Lexy, at eleven, was nearly as big as me. She was really a charming child—with a certain innocence which made us all very protective towards her. She had little of the acute awareness and shrewd insight of the travellers and was untouched by the teasing waves of emotions and vibrations with which I had to struggle. She was more like the 'country hantle', as we called country folk who were not travellers—clever enough at school, but lacking in the acute sense peculiar to travelling people. She and I got on very well together, with none of the clashes which Katie and I always had.

Anyway, we decided to weed the garden and were busily occupied at it when we heard the click of the gate latch. Looking up, who did we see but a priest coming down the path.

I tutted and whispered, 'God pity him.' This was his fourth visit since Father's death and we were beginning to get a bit annoyed with him.

'Good evening, girls,' he greeted us.

'Good evening, sir—Mother isn't in tonight,' I answered.

'I didn't see any of you at chapel on Sunday,' he continued.

Both of us just hung our heads and didn't answer him.

'You really must come to chapel, you know,' he went on. 'You loved your father, didn't you?'

We both nodded.

'Well, then, if you loved him you must come and pray for his soul.'

'But he's dead!' Lexy burst out.

'I know he is dead, dearie. That is why you must come and pray for his sins to be forgiven. Otherwise his soul will be kept in Purgatory.'

'What is Purgatory?' Lexy asked him. Neither of us heard anything about this before.

The priest smiled and said 'It is a place where the souls of the dead are kept in torment and torture until their loved ones pray for them.'

At this Lexy burst into tears and ran into the house.

'Look what you've done! You have frightened my wee sister!' I burst out.

But the priest was unperturbed. 'It is only right that we should fear God,' he answered me.

I had been taught to show respect, but the venom I had been

struggling with flared up at his words and came spitting out of my mouth—brought on by the fierce love which most travelling people have for their kin. I could hear Lexy sobbing hysterically. If he had been the Pope of Rome I couldn't have contained myself.

'You wi' the face like a bap with currants stuck in it. Is that what you get paid for? I thought priests were supposed to be holy and godly men. You have committed more sin since you came here tonight than my father did in his whole life. It's your own soul that you should be praying for. Terrifying weans and telling lies about God!'

On the last words I lifted my eyes and scanned his face—and the venom quickly left me. There was no evil there. This man really believes what he is saying, I thought. So I said, in a quieter voice, 'With respect, sir, you must see that you are the one who is sinning.'

Now it was his turn to get ruffled. 'What else could I expect from an ignorant tinker?' he almost shouted.

At this I threw back my head and laughed—the sort of laughter that is struggling with tears, yet provoked by what seemed to me really funny. I was so certain that he was ignorant and he was just as certain that I was!

'I never tinkered in my life and as for being ignorant—well, I accept that I am ignorant, but no' near as much as you are. I don't go around fearing weans. I'm no' that ignorant.' I was past caring what I said now. Although there was no anger left in me, I somehow felt let down. I had really thought that priests were men of much wisdom and understanding.

'God shall punish you, my girl. You should fear God and ask his forgiveness.' His little black eyes stared into mine as he spoke.

'Dinnae try that on me!' I told him. 'I do fear God—but not in the way that you want me to fear him. God, to me, is all goodness—not the cruel being that you say he is. If he punishes me it'll be as my parents would punish me—and certainly not for what I'm saying to you. You had better hit the road and dinnae come back.'

'I will come back when your mother is in.' He was going

out of the gate as he spoke and, once outside it, he added, 'You need to be taken in hand, young lady.'

I ran into the house and found Lexy on a bed, still breaking her heart crying. She jumped up into my arms, sobbing and saying, 'Daddy! Daddy!'

'What are you greeting for?' I asked her. 'Surely you dinnae believe that silly man?'

She was trembling all over and it took me ever so long to get her calmed down. By the time the others came home she was almost herself again.

We had not meant to tell Mother but she sensed that something was not just right and listened to our tale very quietly, with Lexy on her knee. She shook her head as she looked at me. 'Will you ever learn to keep a calm souch, Betsy? That temper of yours worries me.'

'Well, Ma, I just cannae help it,' I replied.

That night she took Lexy into her bed and Katie and I could hear Mother telling her stories until she fell asleep.

8

For me, however, there was little sleep that night.

My conscience slapped, kicked and punched me unmercifully. 'You shouldn't be cheeking up policemen,' it said, 'nor priests. Nor should you read fortunes. The devil will surely get a hold on you. Have you forgotten your promises to your dead father already? What kind of lassie are you?'

Then I thought about what the priest had said. Could he possibly be right? Who was I to call a priest a liar? Every thought seemed to fly from my head straight to my heart and hit it like the wind hits a windmill—making it beat so rapidly that it really frightened me. So I sat up and crept to the foot of the bed and gently over Katie's feet, then went out of our room quietly and down the lobby to Mother's door.

Turning the door knob very cannily I went in and found Mother lying awake smoking her pipe. By now the light of dawn had returned and as there were no curtains drawn I could see her plainly—and Lexy sleeping at her back. Lifting the blankets at the foot of the bed with her feet, she said 'Get in there, look. I'd some thocht that you would be giving me a visit tonight.'

I took the pillow she was holding out to me and went into the bed at her feet. She took my feet and cuddled them into her bosom, saying, 'Ah, your wee bit plouter o' the day keeps you wakin' at night.'

'I think it was more what that priest said, Ma. I dinnae want to be so wild.'

'Ach, you're no' a' that wild. You'll grow out o' that. It has a lot to do with your age.'

My heart had slowed down already and I found myself yawning.

'Might ye heed priests, lassie,' Mother went on. 'I mind o' your father chasing one for his life. Every night that God sent, this priest came to the camp, wanting to marry us. This was before you were born. We told him that we were married. "Who married you?" says he.

'"We got a minister to marry us at the start of the war," I told him, "so that I could get my allowance."

'"Oh, but you're not really married," says he, "except you get married by a priest."

'Your father could stick him no longer and told him that instead of a marriage there would be a burial if he ever came back aggravating us again.'

I must have fallen asleep at that point—although I don't actually remember dropping off.

9

I was awakened next day by Lexy's peals of laughter, her sadness of the night before forgotten. I had over-slept. So I got up quickly and went to see the cause of Lexy's mirth.

Katie was standing in the middle of the living room like

a sheep from the shears. Her beautiful red hair was almost non-existent. Shorn all over to within an inch of her head.

Instantly my heart went out to her. Although she and I were always throwing hard and sharp words at each other, it was all without malice. We really were more than fond of each other. I had heard her say that a girl who worked in a hairdresser's was going to cut her hair for her. 'Is that what she done to your hair?' I needlessly asked, refraining from laughing. Katie was in tears and very angry.

'Aye, an "Eton crop" she called it. She says that it's all the rage.' Katie's hair was so curly and wiry that she couldn't possibly have it very long.

Travellers hated really short hair. The men often said that a woman without hair was like a brose without salt. At that time if a traveller took ill, they were often put into a poorhouse, where the first thing the staff did was cut their hair. Even in ordinary hospitals it seemed to be the custom, so that very short hair was called a 'poorhouse cut'.

Traveller women took great pride in their long tresses, so you can understand why we were all upset about Katie's haircut. Most women who had had their hair shorn wore a hankie over their heads until it grew again. Poor Katie hated to wear anything on her head. She just couldn't bear having her head covered.

Mother was trying to comfort her when we heard a knock at the door. I went to answer it and found a man named Jamesie Reid standing there. Jamesie was a piper who had often given my father reeds for his pipes. Father had said that this man was one of the best pipers he had ever heard. He was also rather lame, and unable to march. 'I'll get Mother,' I told him.

'It's you that I want to see, lass. Have you played the pipes since you lost your dad?'

'No, Mr Reid, I just couldnae.'

'Now, lass, your father asked me to help you with your piping. It's what he wanted. He was very proud of your playing, you know. You come down to the house this afternoon, and bring your dad's pipes. I know you are used to playing with a valve, and my pipes don't have a valve. I just can't use them.'

After some persuasion I agreed.

As I walked back into the house I thought about my father. So he really had known that he was to leave us. Why hadn't I known, I wondered. I really should have.

Katie had washed her hair and it was in tiny curls all over her head. 'That is really quite nice,' I ventured.

'Aye, it's nice. I'm like a red-haired Abyssinian. I have a good mind to go and tear every hair that she has, out by the roots.'

Then Mother told her, 'Your hair grows like heather, lassie. Within a week it will be quite long again.'

'I'm no gaen oot like this!' Katie disappeared into the bedroom as she spoke, to have a good cry, I guessed.

'What was Mr Reid saying to you?' Mother asked. When I told her all she said was, 'Go and bring the chanter.' Mother could play the chanter herself, but had never tried the pipes.

She started to play a beautiful slow Highland air, and I knew that she was pulling no punches with me. This was the last tune that my father had taught me, and although I had managed to conquer much of the pain of losing him, this made an indescribable shiver vibrate through me. I smothered threatening sobs until they almost smothered me, but they were for Mother not Father. The realisation of what she was putting herself through for me suddenly hit me, as I stood looking at her and listening.

'Ach, ye havenae got the grace-notes right,' I said somewhat over-brightly. 'Give me the chanter.' She did so with a rather relieved and rather dim smile. Then I began to play and at the same time cope with the floods of feelings rushing through me. 'You see, Ma?' I said, jumping up and with mock liveliness changing the tune to *Tiddle Toddle*, tapping my heel in time.

I knew that I had eased her mind about me, but I also knew that she had a long road to go yet. Just then Lexy came running in and seeing me with the chanter sent a look in my direction which penetrated right to the marrow of my

23

bones, then dropped her long, dark, curly eyelashes and ran out again.

Later I asked Lexy to come with me to Mr Reid's house. On the way she said, 'How can you bear to play Daddy's pipes? I really thought that you would miss Daddy more than any of us. You were always with him.'

'Lexy,' I answered, 'my heart is rinnin' ower wi' the pain of losing Daddy. Sometimes it threatens to overwhelm me, and send me rinnin' to some dark cave or something, to lie there greetin' until I joined him. Would you like that? Do you think Daddy would like that? Anyway, Daddy used to say that death was life. I can't understand what he meant, but I'm sure he would like us all to be happy.'

Mr Reid and his wife were more than kind to us. He tuned my father's pipes and had me play *The Highland Wedding*, then started to show me a few rather difficult grace-note settings. Then he played a reel on the chanter which included those notes, one part of which I just couldn't get right. In vain I really tried but just couldn't.

However, and this is the truth, Father came to me in a dream that night. We were both sitting as we were wont to do. 'Listen, Betsy,' he said and played the part that I couldn't on the chanter. Then he did it in the canterach. He cantered it over and over till I got it right.

There was nothing eerie or sorrowful in the dream. It was just like we did when he was alive. The bulk of the dream I could not recall in the morning, only the part about the piping. First thing in the morning I tried it, and knew that it was right.

10

My Uncle Andy, Father's brother, and one of his sons came down from Blairgowrie to see us. We had expected him much sooner but he had been very shaken when Father died.

Soon Johnnie, the son, was singing and joking with us girls and had us all laughing. We all wanted to leave the house with them that very day. But they said that there were as many people gathered around Blairgowrie as could eat every raspberry in the district.

'They are sitting half-starving, waiting for the berries to ripen. If you seen some o' yon poor souls, it would mak' ye greet.' Uncle Andy looked so like Father that I had to look away as he spoke. 'I tell you, weans, you wouldn't get a crust o' bread up there—and it will be a fortnight at least before the berries ripen.'

Mother told him that we were very lucky as far as food was concerned, for all the travellers from around Brechin were up at Blair too. 'Hang on a wee and, if you have any coppers, Betsy will go up the street and scran the shops,' she told him. Then when he had given her five shillings, she put it in my hand saying, 'Hurry now, and see what you can get for that. Take Lexy with you.'

We did hurry and soon returned laden. Several loaves of bread baked that day and even cakes; butter which had gone yellow and neep-tasted; dollops of hard cheese; fruit which was just on the turn—and even butcher meat which would not keep for another day, but was still eatable.

Uncle Andy was amazed. 'No wonder you stay here, Maggie,' he said.

'That's how so many travellers stay around here,' she told him. 'If you have a penny at all you would never starve— but it is gey hard to get a penny.'

He wanted us to keep all the food but Mother said, 'Where could we eat all that? It would just be wasted.' So they left with most of it, promising to return for us in a fortnight.

When they left, I turned to Mother. 'Ma, how did you take Uncle Andy's money? Have you no money?' I had just remembered that she had sold the bracelet.

'Not me, lassie. Where was I going to get money?'

'For the bracelet,' I answered her.

'Oh, did I not tell you? I swapped it for a tent, the barriest

25

tent that you ever seen. Come down to the shed and I will
show it to you.'

The tent was good with a bell-shaped back.

11

Sunday was a lovely sunny day so Lexy and I went down to the
river, where most of the Brechin children went in summer. We
knew the place where we would find company, young boys
and girls who used to live beside us in the old slum houses
of Wallace Lane and the Vennel. None of these children were
real traveller children, but their parents had copied travellers,
and had learned from them, in order to get a bite.

Some of their fathers were poachers, and often went to jail
for it. Father had taught one man to make wooden washing
tubs out of old barrels. These tubs were used in almost every
wash-house. Mother had taught women to make sweet peas
and other flowers. In those days young teenagers got nothing
to keep them. There was no dole unless you had stamps and
when the stamps ran out the money was stopped and that was
it. The parish could only cope with householders or the infirm
except in rare cases. So many of these poor folk knew real hunger, more so than travelling people did. I can remember how
some of the boys used to harry small birds' nests and eat the
eggs raw or rather suck them; how they would eat fruit out of
the midden and spoiled sweets which shops had thrown out.

Travellers would rake a midden for scrap metal—lead,
brass, copper or zinc—or even rags, but would never ever
eat anything out of it.

Yet those children or their folks rarely would steal, or
commit other crimes. Poaching was not considered as stealing,
and the South Esk river was well stocked with salmon. So
there was lots of poaching going on. Travellers rarely poached
and never with non-travellers. Scaldies, as we called them,
were less afraid of police and authority. Travellers were
terrified of 'the authorities', mostly because of their habit

of taking away children. There was also another reason: the closing down of camping sites.

Lexy and I found 'the gang', as we called them, just where we expected to—between the river and the lade near the Dennies. The Dennies is a sort of dell with a little burn winding through it, wooded and lush with wild flowers, broom and briar trees. I loved this place where I had played with the gang often the lee-lang summer's day—building tree houses, playing hide-and-seek, Jocky-the-lum, and many other games.

However, I must get back to the gang. Lexy and I could hear the sough of them before we could see them. They were all laughing like to split, except one girl who was standing in the middle of the river. We were soon told that her knickers had become transparent when they got wet, and she couldn't come out of the water because of the hilarious laughter of the boys, and the girls were just as bad.

One of the boys had a whippet which had caught a rabbit. The rabbit had been skinned, washed in the burn, and cooked on a piece of grid-iron above a fire. Now they were pulling it apart and eating it, shouting, 'Come on out, Hattie! Hurry up or it will be all eaten!' to the girl in the water. Hattie swore and made many impossible threats as they taunted her by holding out pieces of savoury-smelling, though saltless, rabbit.

In the end, of course, someone did throw Hattie a towel, and a piece of the rabbit was kept for her.

They were a great bunch of youngsters, nearly all in their teens. The two eldest boys were over eighteen, a boy called Billy Middleton and another one name of Paddy Reilly. They, weary of the life without work, money and sometimes even food, had joined the Forces. Paddy had applied to the Argyll and Sutherlands. Billy had received his papers back and would soon be joining a ship in the Navy.

Lexy was soon into the water, but I was nearly sixteen, and no traveller girl of that age would dare be seen half-naked in front of boys. We were not allowed even to wear a dress without sleeves, or go bare-legged. So I sat and played cards with some of the gang, including Hattie's older sister Nora,

who was going into service—a missionary lady had found
her a job in a hotel in Perth. There were about twelve of us
altogether, and the younger boys were eager to grow older
so that they also could join up. It seemed the only possible
way to eat regularly and get clothed.

We spent a happy day there and then went home knowing
that we would all see each other again in the morning when
the strawberry picking was starting.

I 2

We saw them all right, and hundreds more, as we made our
way out to the Louchlands farm early the next morning,
so many young people desperate to earn a few pennies.
Some had been out at the farm since the back of six in
the morning. As Mother said, 'There's enough folk here to
eat all the strawberries in the field.'

Of course there were folk of all ages there, but the sight of
so many youngsters was to Mother rather depressing. 'God
help us aa. We think oursels bad, but when you see a sicht
like that.' She was looking at a woman with four pale, thin,
ill-clad weans as she spoke. 'We can mak' some shift for
oursels, but they poor craturs cannae. Look at that young
lad over there. His face is cutting the wind. That lassie, she
has devil tae a haet aneath that auld overall. Aye, it's a queer
world. Even if they could get work now, I doubt if mony o'
them would hae the fushion tae dae it. Ah weel, what can a
body dae?' Then her tone changed. 'Run, lassies, and get a
dreel before they are all taken.'

We earned about a sixpence each that day, two and a half
pence in today's money. However, before the end of the week
there were plenty strawberries for everyone. Picking them all
day can be a sair job, but when you have also to grade them
as well, it is doubly so. Only perfect berries were accepted. All
the others had to be put into what was called a brock-basket.
This really slowed you down.

Poor Mother found it almost impossible. She somehow crushed the berries and was always having them rejected, and getting severely reprimanded from the weigh-man.

Dinner time was from half past eleven until one o'clock, and all work stopped then. This was because the ploughmen had to unyoke and feed their horses, then reyoke and let them drink before starting work again. The farmer's wife always had a large iron kettle full of boiling water ready, and would also heat pies in her oven for anyone lucky enough to have them.

Mother had a very large milk-can which we got filled with tea. No way would she drink tea out of a vacuum flask.

We were just sitting taking our dinner when who should come along but an old woman who went around selling lavender. She came of travelling people, but being widowed young had travelled from town to town, lodging house to lodging house, sometimes 'singing the streets', too independent to live with relatives.

Seeing Mother, she came over to us. 'Oh, it's yoursel', Jean,' Mother greeted her, 'I didnae ken you were in this side of the countrie. Sit down and get a drink o' tea, and gie us a crack.'

'Aye, Maggie, its been a lang time, and Sandy's awa'. Is this your lassies? They were just weans when I last saw them. Are you picking berries?'

'Strawberries,' Mother answered.

'I cannae mind when I last tasted a strawberry,' Jean said.

'Would you like some?' I asked her.

'I could dae fine wi twa or three. You're Betsy aren't you? A young woman already.'

'I'll run and get some,' I told her.

Away I went back towards the strawberry field. All the pickers were at the farm sitting in wee groups taking their dinner. So the big field was empty. The farmer was very strict about taking his berries, so I made sure no one was in sight when I picked up a basket and began filling it.

It was a lovely day, and my mind wandered as it was wont to do. I had scarcely time to coax it back completely when I glanced around on hearing a deep voice shouting, 'And what's going on here?' I glimpsed the figure of a man throwing down a bicycle and start running down the drill towards me. The farmer, I thought, throwing down the basket and taking off like a hare.

I really could run, but I could hear the footsteps getting closer behind me. So I turned around and saw that it was a traveller boy whom I knew slightly. 'You silly galoot!' I shouted, and immediately started to pick up stones and throw them at him.

'Ca' canny, lassie. I was just making a bit o' fun with you,' he shouted back.

'Fun!' I roared, 'Funny kind o' fun that.'

'Man but you're a wild yin!' He was dodging the stones as he spoke. 'You could dae damage tae a body with that stones.'

'If I dinnae it'll no' be for want o' trying,' I answered.

By now he was running up the field and me after him throwing every stone that I could find. 'Weel ye might run, Squirrel, because I will beat you into atoms if I do catch you.'

'A squirrel is better than a grumfie's lugs!' he roared back. 'No, laddie, a squirrel is no half as good as a grumfie's dung. You never sooked the milk, laddie.'

I think that I should explain here about this 'Grumfie' and 'Squirrel' exchange. All travellers have a family nickname, and at that time they got very angry indeed if any other traveller shouted their nickname. I have seen a camping ground like a modern-day football match, so strongly did they feel about nicknames. How families came to get those nicknames is a mystery. None of them know. At that time travellers were a bit like the old Scottish clans, and if you met a young person you could tell at once whether he was a Burke, Stewart, McKenzie, or whatever. They seldom married outside their own 'breed' as they called them. I have often been told, on meeting some traveller whom I had never seen before, 'You are a Johnstone, or if not there is a good bit of a Johnstone in you.'

However let's go back to the strawberry field. The young man that I had been pelting with stones was called Bryce Whyte, and the Whyte's nickname is 'the Squirrels', and mine is 'Grumfie's Lugs.' A grumfie, if you haven't guessed, is the animal that grunts.

Anyway, he was away up near the top of the field, now looking back and grunting loudly. I could do no more than shake my fists at him. The path along the top of the field was a short cut from one farm to another, and Bryce had been going to the farm bothies at dinner-time to sell things like leather laces, razor-blades, studs, etc. There could be eight or nine or even more men in a bothy, so with luck a couple of bothies was better than a whole day going round the cottar houses.

I too decided to take a short cut back to the farm across the fields. So I hurriedly picked up a basket—they were lying all over the field—and half filled it with strawberries. Then I went through the paling and started towards the farm.

Now in this field there was a large knowe covered with broom and whin bushes. I climbed up the knowe, but when I got to the top and looked down, my heart shifted. I was looking down in the eyes of an entire (the term horsemen use for an ungelded horse, a stallion). I saw his ears go back, and the forward thrust of his neck. So once again the strawberries got a throw, as I scrambled down the knowe and I'm sure the sparks were flying from my feet as I made for the paling. Now, it was a barbed wire paling, then a ditch half full of water, then another barbed wire paling. Somehow I reached it before the entire and flung myself over it. Then into the ditch, and up and through the other paling.

I was back into the strawberry field, where I threw myself down breadth and length on my back gasping for breath. I was never one to scream, but Bryce must have noticed my mad race, and had come running to help me but was a bit late. I knew that he would have faced the entire. I had seen him handling young horses. He reached me minutes after I got through the fence. 'Are you all right?' he asked, kneeling beside me.

My throat was as dry as a match-stick, so I could only nod, then close my eyes and wait for my heart to slow its mad tattoo.

Bryce put a strawberry to my lips and I willingly opened my mouth for it. He popped another one in after a few minutes, and kept doing this till I could speak again. 'You ken, you look bonnier than ever lying down like that,' I heard him say. So I quickly opened my eyes and scanned his face, then relaxed and closed them again, knowing that I was as safe with him as I would be with a new-born lamb.

Soon I was able to sit up, and when I looked down at myself I started to laugh. My dungarees were torn and I was covered in wet earth. The back of my blouse was stuck in the barbed wire waving like a flag. Knots of my long hair too were caught in the barbed wire, like sheep's wool.

'What are you laughing at?' Bryce asked.

'You,' I told him, 'saying I was bonnie, in a mess like this.'

'You are,' he answered, 'but a wild yin. My legs are black and blue with the stones.'

'Well that was your own fault. I hate folk that think ill-getted tricks are funny.'

I rose up and looked across the fences to where the stallion was strutting about majestically. 'If he wasn't so big he would get the same dose,' I told Bryce. Then once again I got a basket and started putting some berries into it.

'I will help you,' Bryce said. 'You've not long lost your father,' he ventured.

'Aye', was all I could answer, 'and you lost a sister.'

Then he began to tell me about the sister who had died over in Aberdeenshire. 'She had been ailing for a while,' he continued. 'I used to, if I could get the coppers, take her home fruit or something. I miss her terribly. She used to read to me at nights.' Noticing that the basket was full, I straightened up and saw that his eyes were full of tears. Mine remained dry—my grief was beyond tears.

We had reached the top of the field. 'I must run,' I told him, as he picked up his bike.

'Wait, and I'll walk along with you.'

'No, you get on the bike and I'll run.'

'I thought you would have had enough of running for one day,' I could hear him mutter as he complied.

13

We reached the farm at the same time. Mother took one look at me and asked, 'What happened this time?'

Now there were several groups of non-travellers sitting within ear-shot. So mostly for their benefit I exclaimed loudly, 'Oh, Ma, it was this laddie here. He raped me in the strawberry field.'

Mother glanced up at Bryce whose face had gone redder than the tail light of his bicycle. 'Come and sit down, laddie, and get a mouthful of tea. It's no very warm now but there's some sandwiches left too.' I knew that Bryce would have been transparent to Mother, in the light of the new moon.

However I did hear murmurings from the non-travellers and one woman say, 'Ee, isn't that awful? Fancy giving him tea and him after raping her lassie.'

They thought so little of us that I felt a strange delight in making myself even worse than they thought. I knew that Bryce could have done with a word with me before he left, but I gave him no chance.

Auld Jean was delighted with the strawberries and said with a glisk in her eyes, 'They were worth waiting for.'

'I think I'll daunder down the road with you, Jean,' Mother said. 'I can do nothing to please that man like a black snail, wha weighs the berries. I would be better gaen hame and yoking the pony. The poor animal is bound to be wearied standing in the stable all day.'

'Be sure and take Ricky too, Ma,' I told her.

'Aye, aye, I ken that. Awa and wash your face, lassie, but

no' in the horse's trough. You could get ring-worm. Wash it at the speekit.'

'That's an affie lassie,' I heard her say to auld Jean as they started to walk down the road. Katie and Lexy had been for a walk and when they saw me on returning they both stared, then laughed hilariously. 'If you could only see yoursel,' Lexy said. 'What in the name of God have you been doing?'

'Give me a loan of your comb,' I asked her, whilst trying to dry my face with a head-square.

'What tore the leg of your trousers?' Katie put in, 'and look at your blouse!' As I tried to explain, their laughter became almost hysterical.

'Where's Mother?' Lexy asked. I told her.

Back in the berry field I could hear a lot of snickering behind my back from the other pickers. The worst thing, however, was the attitude of the middle-aged gaffer who walked about the field making sure that no one left berries. 'Fits this ye were up to at denner-time then? Did ye like it? Eh?' Looking at the tremble of his hands and the leer on his face, my stomach whammelled. When he bent down to semi-whisper, 'Fit are ye dee-en the night?' I almost hit him.

'I'll tell you what I'm doing,' I answered him. 'I am going inbye to see your wife.'

He made a hasty retreat then.

14

'There is a letter on the mantelpiece,' Mother told us when we got home. Mother could neither read nor write. The letter was from Uncle Andy. He wrote that his son Johnnie had acquired an old car and that he would be coming down to take us up to the raspberry picking on the following Saturday. 'I will take the horse myself,' Andy informed us. He too was illiterate, but not his family.

When I got up on Saturday morning, day was just returning from night whose old grey plaid still hung over her. I knew it must be very early indeed, but Lexy too was up. We were so excited about getting away to the country. 'You are all very clever this morning,' Mother said when she got up later—to find that we had done all the necessary packing, and cleaned and dusted everything. 'Anyone would think that we were going for a cruise on the *Queen Mary*,' Mother went on. Lexy and I were singing and frolicking about, but Katie was very quiet. We knew that she was worried about her lack of hair.

We didn't have a clock. We rarely needed one, preferring just to do everything in God's own time. Eating when we felt hungry, and doing things when we had a notion to. We hated the frustration of any work which started and finished at a set time, so avoided it if possible. Travelling people will do any really hard work speedily and well, if allowed to do it in their own way, so they mostly did piece-work.

We didn't have to wait long for cousin Johnnie and his father. They must have been up very early too. Uncle Andy set off first with Prince. He could not drive a car. The rest of us and our few belongings were soon packed into Johnnie's old bottle-nosed Morris Cowley. We talked, laughed and sang on our journey up, passing Uncle Andy at Careston.

The camping-place was at the side of a hayfield. Hay, and all other crops, were harvested much later then than they are nowadays, and the hay was still drying in little stacks called ricks. Many of Mother's relations she hadn't seen for years, and which we her daughters had never seen, were there. They had come down from the highlands of Perthshire to try to keep Mother's heart up after the loss of Father.

The farmer had provided an ex-army bell-tent for us and some of the young lads had erected it. A lot of berry farmers kept bell-tents for the berry-pickers. All the rest of them had their own bow tents. Two girl cousins had been to the farm for bunches of straw, which we rummled and crumpled before making our beds with it. Introductions were made all around, amidst much hugging and exchanging of admiration. The sight of so many male cousins made me feel for Mother. My two brothers had died in early childhood, and male children were almost a necessity amongst travelling people at that time.

The familiar smells of clover, burning wood and the hay made me close my eyes and breathe deeply—desperately trying to keep thoughts of Daddy from my mind. The sight of so many little by-ways and fields where I had walked and worked with him really scalded my heart.

15

The sound of peculiar piping reached my ears and I rushed out of the tent, where I had been making the beds, and saw a sight which chased all the melancholy thoughts of Father from my mind. My cousin Hendry's wee boy, no more than seven years old, was playing the smallest set of bagpipes that I had ever seen. His fair curls were bobbing on his brow and his wee pink fingers were rattling out *Highland Laddie*. His timing was perfect. Something which was almost a pain hit my heart as I listened. His mother stood looking on with love and pride in her eyes. She was a McDonald, married to one of Uncle Jimmy's sons.

'I would never have believed anyone telling me that a wean of his age could play like that,' I told her. 'Oh me, lassie, that laddie has been blowing a chanter since he was two years old. Your Uncle Jimmy, his grandfather, has him conyeeched to death. He bought they wee pipes for him, and a Highland outfit made to measure, and sits for hours and hours teaching him, and making reeds for his wee chanter.' She went into her tent and came out with a tiny practice chanter, saying, 'Look what he had made for him.' Her name was Jean and wee Tommy the piper was the eldest of her three children.

Mother too was very taken with wee Tommie's piping. 'He is fairly his Granda's bairn,' she said.

Mother and my aunts got to talking together about old times. Katie and the other older girls had made supper. Lexy was playing with other bairns. So after washing the dishes

I decided to slip away on my own. This was a habit of mine which often annoyed and even worried Mother. Yet this was something which I could not bear to be without. To be alone and yet to escape even from myself, into the undescribable world of nature. I could actually feel it as I looked around me at her beauty. What I felt was that I was in the presence of some wonderful mystic power completely outwith this world. Could it be God? Anyway I had never found a kindred spirit in this. So I just had to be alone.

However I was not going to get the chance that day. I had barely reached the old road which ran along the top of the berry-fields when I was confronted with one of my male cousins—one of Uncle Geordie's sons who I had never met until that day. He was about nineteen, big, and very handsome, and very much aware of it. He stood confidently looking down on me. I could detect arrogance, and a certain restless vibration, a pulsating explosiveness if you like, in his personality.

'Well, well, and what are you doing away up here on your own?' he asked.

Almost immediately I could feel the fire in my own nature surface. 'Minding my own business,' I answered, 'and I'd thank you to do the same.'

'The minute that I saw you step out of Johnnie's car today, I decided that from then on you *were* going to be my business,' he told me.

'Oh, did you now? Well I'm sorry, laddie, but you can just run away home again. I don't need a collie dog. I already have one.' Ricky of course had followed me and was poking about in the undergrowth.

'You are a right impudent, fiery wee bitch,' he went on, 'but I'll soon sort that out.'

'What will you do?' I shouted. 'Ho, laddie! You would like to get the chance, but I'm sorry, you never will.' With that I took off back towards the tents, Ricky at my heels.

The older generation were in the mood for a celebration. So little Tommy's father, who had an old van, was just getting his orders from them on what to go and fetch from the town.

'Don't forget sweeties and lemonade for the weans, and some bottles of stout for the young women,' Uncle Duncan was saying, 'and tobacco.'

When Hendry left I sat down beside his wife Jean and asked her the name of Uncle Geordie's youngest son. 'Ah,' she answered, 'so you have noticed him already. All the young girls fall for Willie. A real bonny laddie isn't he?'

'I'm not falling for him. In fact I don't think that I even like him,' I told her.

'Aye, aye, so you're saying. I believe you.' Her tone, however, made it clear that she did not believe me.

16

Hendry returned with a sack of beer and whisky amongst other things, and soon the merriment began. Piping was *the* thing with the Johnstones, my mother's people. Almost all the males could play, and some of them were truly great pipers.

Of course I was asked to play, and received more praise than enough. Very few of the young ones would take any drink, but sang for their parents or danced to the pipes. A great deal of heart-to-heart talking went on too. It was lucky that we were miles away from anywhere, the nearest house being the farm which was about six hundred yards away.

About one o'clock in the morning they were beginning to tire. Then talk got up about my father and tears began to flow. I was rather disturbed by this as I had never heard grown men cry. The sight of bairns comforting crying grannies and grandads was somehow very moving. The young ones showed an almost fierce protectiveness towards their parents, guarding them from the fire or from falling, and coaxing them with food, which was always refused.

Hendry, however, got really hungry at about two o'clock in the morning when there was nothing cooked left to eat. Jean, his wife, had gone to bed with the bairns and he was shouting at her to get up and fry sausages and eggs for him. When she refused he started to pull her out of bed, making all kinds of threats to her. He had taken a lot of drink.

'What's going on here?' his father asked. Uncle Jimmie still had his senses. 'Listen, mannie, if I see you lay one hand on that lassie, I'll kick you round all this field.'

'He has taken the whisky hunger,' Jean said, 'and would I fry sausages and eggs to him at this time of morning.'

'Get into your bed, man,' his father told him.

Hendry didn't answer his father, but ran into his old van, and started the engine. However, instead of making for the road he started to run the van into the hay ricks, backing out of the one and then running into another through all the field until he ended up exhausted slumped over the wheel. He was soon pulled from the van and bedded.

There was no bed that night for the young ones, who were more than just busy repairing the ricks. Jean too helped and talked as we worked about other silly ploys which Hendry had done before. Most of us knew how to build a hay stack but in the semi-dark, and with only one graip, it was no easy task. If the farmer or grieve knew, we would get our walking tickets very fast. Luckily this was a Sunday morning and we didn't start working until Monday. So we kept at it until we were satisfied no-one would notice. By then the older ones were all up. Most of them were asking for bandanas which they tied tightly round their heads, until they looked like a puckle of wild Indians. They were also draining the whisky bottles which, alas, were all empty. The idea of the bandanas was that they were convinced that the tight pressure round the heads stopped, or at least eased, their headaches.

Jean, who had brought her sense of humour to her aid that early morning, was in a rather cantankerous mood now. Hendry was still sleeping while she, without any sleep all night, had to cope with a baby and two other small children. 'Are you going to rise, Rab Ha'? That's wha you're like— the Glesga Glutton, him that ate the hundred-weight o' tripe. Dinnae think that you are gaen tae lie there aa day after making sure that nobody else got babbin' an eye!' Jean was really in a rage.

Hendry ignored her, so she threw off all the stones which secured the tent-cover and pulled the cover right off, leaving him lying with only the tent-sticks above him. However, he only happed his head with the blankets and snuggled under them.

Just then someone spotted the figures of two men coming across the next field. One of them was a policeman, the other in civilian clothes. Everyone dived into their tents, except Jean of course—she had no cover on hers. Anyway she was so wild with Hendry that she couldn't have cared less. I decided to stay with her, as I was holding her baby. I am sure that they all thought that the police had come about the hay ricks.

I noticed the policeman's smile as he eyed the coverless tent. The other well-dressed man was looking all around him a bit apprehensively. 'Hello, lass,' the policeman greeted Jean. 'We have just come to take your census.'

'Senses?' Jean shouted. 'Did you say senses, constable? Well, I doot ye have come tae the wrang place for that. Naebody here has ony sense tae themselves.' Now I knew that Jean was quite an intelligent girl and that this talk was all to annoy Hendry.

'Na, na, lass. I just want to ken your names and the date o' your births, whar you were born and so on.'

'I cannae tell ye that either, mister. The only thing I can tell ye is that it is a pity that I ever was born.' I could see Hendry squirm underneath the blankets. The police too had noticed. He had guessed the situation and was really enjoying it. The other man, however, was sure that he had come to an open asylum. 'If you want to ken onything like that, you will hae tae ask my man. He is lying in there, look, underneath the cloots. Rab's his name. Rab Ha'.'

Grinning widely, the constable went to where Hendry was lying and shook him, saying, 'Come on, Rab. Tak' your head oot o' the blankets. I'm needing tae tak' your census.'

Hendry curled the blankets more tightly around him, but the constable grabbed them and pulled them off his head.

'Canny, min! I'm naked!' Hendry cried. 'If I could only find my auld troosers, I'd gie ye senses. It's senseless I'd mak' ye, you and her baith. Polis or no polis. I couldnae care less this morning, if I were to get seven years in Barlinnie.'

He then started to cackle like a hen and put his head up and down like a hen pecking. The good-natured policeman was now laughing heartily, as were me and Jean. Of course the policeman didn't know why Hendry was imitating a hen, but Jean and I did. The Hens was the nickname of her breed of McDonalds, their family nickname.

Hendry was still at it. The man who was with the constable hadn't uttered a sound. He just stood there in dazed confusion. 'Well, well, I think we'll away and let you twa simmer doon.' The policeman turned to me as he spoke. 'What about your folk, lass?'

'They are aa in the doldrums o' drink, constable. Could you possibly come back tomorrow evening, when they are at their senses again?' I laughingly answered him. He also laughed and nodded. What a fine man, I thought. I was sure that he must have had acquaintance with travelling people.

As soon as they were out of sight, all the others spewed out of the tents. There was much laughter and questions. Hendry had found his trousers and he and Jean were on the best of terms within minutes. Their sense of humour had smothered their anger.

17

The next few days found us working hard at the rasp-picking. Few of our cousins had ever picked rasps before. The older folks just worked when they felt like it, all of the children and young folk gave whatever they earned to their parents. 'You can all keep what you earn on Friday,' we were told, 'and you can go into Blairgowrie on Saturday. I want Hendry to come into the town and bring you home again. He'll have to make two journeys.'

So come Saturday we were excited about going to Blairgowrie. Willie's sister Ann and I had become good friends. We went for walks together, picked berries together, and never tired of each other's company. The only thing that spoiled it was my attitude towards her brother. She idolized Willie and couldn't believe that I didn't admire him. Ann was great fun to be with. Everything was so new to her. She had never been further down the country than Pitlochry, and she had never been inside a picture-house. So just to watch her face enjoying things was a treat. Blairgowrie at the berry-time was like a wonderland to her. So many different travellers, scores of horses and carts, lined the Well-meadow. Hundreds of berry-pickers from Dundee, Glasgow, Fife and many other places, came into Blairgowrie on a Saturday. There used to be a camping ground just before you crossed the bridge going into Blair, behind the billboards. There were shows there, a fair, with a cake-walk, a helter-skelter, a boxing booth and many other attractions. Ann was speechless as we walked around, but was a bit wary of going on anything.

Feeling a tap on my shoulder I turned to find Bryce Whyte. He was with a pal. His family were on a farm near Alyth, he told me. 'Come, and I'll pay you on the chair-o-planes,' he asked, but no way would Ann go on them.

'Come on to the cake-walk, Ann,' I pleaded. She finally agreed, and enjoyed it, also the helter-skelter.

'There is a good picture on tonight,' Bryce said later. 'Are you going?'

'Yes!' Ann said, very enthusiastically. 'I've never been to the pictures.'

'That's fine,' Bryce said, 'then I will see you there.'

'Not me,' I told him, 'I will have to go home with Mother.' I didn't want Willie to see Bryce, and I'd rather have missed the pictures than have Willie enraged. He had become more persistent every day, and truly believed that I was playing hard to get.

'But you promised,' Ann said. Then, thinking that I didn't want to see Bryce, 'You and I both promised to keep an eye on the auld yins.'

Bryce was a bit down on hearing this. 'Where are you staying?' he asked.

'We are shifting tomorrow!' I shouted back as we walked away.

'When will I see you?' he ran after us shouting.

'When we get back to Brechin!' I shouted back.

It suited me fine that Ann thought that I wanted rid of Bryce, because she had seen me rebuffing her brother. So Ann didn't get to the pictures that night. She was disappointed but wouldn't go without me. We walked home instead. We loved long walks, passing other berry places packed with tents. We took a short cut across fields on the last lap as it were. We talked all the time, and ran and laughed.

18

Then we heard corncrakes chirming, dismally I thought.

The day seemed to darken despite the absence of cloud. Strange waves of emotion hit me, making me tense and tremble. 'Let's sit a minute, Ann,' I said.

'No,' she answered, 'I have a queer feeling that I must get home quickly. I just know that something is wrong.'

So Ann too is cursed with this, I thought, but refrained from telling her of my fears.

We cleeked together and ran across the fields. Ricky ran to meet us whimpering in protest because I had left him all day. Mother was standing alone beside the fire. Fearfully I lifted my eyes to meet hers. For a brief moment she returned my look, then her eyes shifted to Ann. 'Tell me quickly, Auntie Maggie, quickly.'

Mother moved towards her, saying, 'It's your sister Elsie. The polis were here to tell us. She was rushed to Perth hospital but they couldn't save her. Milk fever, they think.'

Ann's first thoughts were for her parents. 'My Daddy and Mammy?' She sobbed the question.

'Sleeping,' Mother told her. 'Jean has taken all the weans

43

for a walk. Hendry is away in to Blair to find all the rest of them.'

Elsie was only nineteen when she died. Her husband's folk stayed at Pitlochry.

Hendry soon returned with Aunt Martha and Uncle Geordie's family. Willie ran to Ann; his first thoughts too were for his parents. I was looking at a very different Willie. Grief had softened him. Katie and another cousin of her age were also in the van. My other four uncles and their wives came out of their tents, when their families came home, and began to pull down their tents.

Before ten o'clock that night we were all on our way to Pitlochry. Hendry had taken Uncle Geordie and his wife and family and as many as he could pack into his van. There were four yokes as well so all of us got piled into them. We travelled most of the night trying to go through Dunkeld as quietly as possible. Elsie had married a boy named Sutherland and had been living in a quarry near Pitlochry.

Aunt Martha was sitting with her dead daughter's baby on her knee. With her was the baby's other granny and some younger women. The baby was just three days old. The baby's father was there too, completely dazed, just sitting on a tree-stump staring with unseeing eyes.

Jean had already fed the motherless infant, she being the only woman with a very young child. She would continue to feed it until it was weaned.

Aunt Martha, however, would rear the baby. This was understood. She had lost her daughter and the child would help to ease the pain of this. The baby's father or his mother would make no protest, for it was the way of travelling people. They do not believe in step-parents, and it was also understood that young Peter, the baby's father who was only twenty-one, would in time marry again.

It is very rare indeed that a traveller child has a step-parent. If there was a childless sister, brother, aunt, cousin or whoever, young children were given to them to rear when a parent remarried. The natural parent would not interfere in their upbringing, nor would they be expected to give anything towards the child's keep. Sometimes a four- or five-year-old was even given a choice. 'Daddy is going to get married again, son. Who would you like to go and live with?' It didn't matter if the relative chosen had ten of his or her own already. No traveller woman would refuse a child for there is absolutely nothing that can bring more happiness. Yet there was and still is this thing about step-parents. Their passionate love of children was perhaps the reason for it.

Elsie was buried in Little Dunkeld. Hundreds of travelling people attended the funeral. Many of them stayed over and most of them got drunk that night, and the next and the next night. They stayed until their money was done then, after prolonged sentimental farewells, went off to their own camping places.

The young girls looked after the bairns and cooked and washed. The young men and boys attended to the horses, fetched firewood, and looked after their parents and other older relatives.

Mother too was part of this drinking binge and, as my father had been a non-drinker, she had rarely indulged before his death. So Lexy, Katie and I were truly lost and rather upset seeing her drunk. There was no feeling of the security of a mother's presence. Now I knew why they called it spirits, I thought. This person was a spirit of drink. Not my real mother.

However, it cost money and that was all gone within a week. One morning Mother, looking terrible, said, 'I'm dead this morning. I'll never put that cursed drink in my mouth again.' She was ryping her pockets as she spoke. 'Betsy, run and see if ony o' them has an inch o' tobacco to give me.' None of them had. Not a haet, nor any money to buy some. 'God pity the drink,' Mother said.

Then wee Tommie came running to our tent. 'Betsy, Grandad wants you,' he said. When I reached Uncle Jimmie's tent he had dressed and was up, but he looked even worse than Mother.

'Dochter, will you do something for your auld uncle?' he asked me.

'Aye, surely, Uncle, what do you want me tae dae?'

'Look at me, daughter,' he said holding out his hands. He was shaking like a leaf with the power of the doldrums of drink. His eyes were blood-shot, and his face like chalk. 'Curse the drink,' he went on. 'I can hardly stand let alone play my pipes. Be a good wee lassie and tak' my auld drones wi' ye into the toon and play to some o' them gentry. I'm gaen tae dee, dochter, if I dinnae get a smoke. They laddies winnae gang—they laddies wouldnae care if I was tae dee.'

'Oh no, Uncle!' I cried. 'I couldnae!'

'Look, tak' wee Tommy wi' ye. Aa you'll hae tae dae is stand there beside him. He's no shy. Dae that for me, and I'll never forget ye.'

I just couldn't refuse him. So Jean, who didn't touch drink other than the daily bottle of stout which the others forced upon her, soon got wee Tommy ready. The reason for making Jean take the stout was to nourish her while she fed two bairns, and to make milk in her breasts.

19

Anyway, away Tommy and I went. It was no distance to Pitlochry. The minute that we hit the town, the eyes of every passer-by was on him. Jean had put on his little made-to-measure Highland outfit, and he really was something to look at. We went to a place where the touring buses stopped and there Tommy started to play. He was really enjoying it, not being encumbered with my shy backwardness.

I placed his little glengarry bonnet down on the ground, to prevent me having go round with it in the hope of getting a few coppers. Some people had gathered to listen and one or two had thrown a halfpenny or a penny into the bonnet.

Then a coach came in and all the passengers got out. They were immediately attracted to the piping and the piper. I soon realised that they were English and that, for most of them, Tommy and his pipes were great novelties.

One man amongst them was acting as spokesman, and all went well until I heard him say 'They live in the woods you know. In ugly little tents. Very dirty, lazy people. They make and mend things for a living, but more often steal what they need.' He talked as if I was deaf. Or that I was too dense to understand him.

Never had my blood come to boiling point more quickly. My heart too was coming dunts off my ribs, but I gripped my tongue between my teeth. It strived against me, but I held on tight.

The man who was the cause of my rage had gone over to Tommy and was shouting in his ear. Then he turned to me and asked, 'Can he play *Culloden Moor*?'

Well, if my hackles had been up before, they were sky high now. '*Culloden Moor*!' I almost screamed, thinking to myself, I'll give the English puddock *Culloden Moor* and *Flodden Field* all in one dish. With great effort I managed to answer him. 'Tommy disnae ken that one, but I will play it for you.' Then I hurriedly extracted Uncle Jimmie's pipes from their box, swung them onto my shoulder and played a very spirited if rather unskilled rendering of *Johnny Cope*.

Anger had overcome shyness, and I stomped about like a midden-cock. Twice over I played it until I had stamped some of the overpowering power of anger out through my feet. Then I stopped, and almost immediately someone gave me a gulder of a roar which nearly shifted the hearts of all the gathering.

It came from a local policeman who had been standing looking on and listening. He came over towards me, shouting, 'Well done, my bonny wee lassie!' That's the best I've heard for mony a lang day.' He was slapping his thigh and laughing like to burst.

I knew that he wasn't referring to my piping, but most of the onlookers thought he was. Another elderly gentleman came over to me and said, 'Very well done, lass! Very, very, well done!' He was a local man.

The policeman had picked up Tommy's bonnet, and was going round the crowd holding it out to them. 'Come on, folks! Out wi' your coppers. You've never heard the like o' that before, and you're no' likely ever to hear it again.'

The man who had asked for the tune was standing smiling broadly and looking down on me with twinkling eyes. I had never really looked at him face on until now. He was slowly shaking his head. He doesn't look such a bad being, really, I thought. The policeman came over to him holding out the bonnet, saying, 'You called the tune, mister, now pay the piper.'

'She certainly deserves to be paid,' the man answered, dropping a piece of silver into Tommy's glengarry. 'There is, however, something I must tell you. I am Scottish myself although I was reared in England, and I can play a bit on the pipes too.'

The policeman and I felt a bit crestfallen when we heard this.

Then the two men started to laugh heartily, and shake each other by the hand. 'Just the same I wouldn't have missed this for a fiver,' the policeman said, as he came over and handed me the bonnet. 'There you are, lass, you have done all right for yourselves. You can retire for the day now.'

The other man too came over to me, saying, 'Thank you for the entertainment. It was worth coming to Scotland, if only to experience this. Can I too shake hands with you?'

My shyness had returned and I could only mumble, 'Yes sir, thank you, sir.' But I hadn't entirely forgotten his description of the travelling people. That still rankled.

There were quite a few silver pieces amongst the coppers in the bonnet. I lifted some out, then put the bonnet inside Uncle Jimmie's pipe box, beside his pipes.

'Tommy, will you stand here and look after the pipe boxes whilst I run to the shop.'

'Mind and bring me something back,' he answered.

'Surely,' I told him as I sped away.

Two ounces of tobacco was my first purchase, then sweets for Tommy. Then I found a butcher's shop, and when I went in the old gentleman who had spoken to me earlier was standing there talking to the butcher. 'Well, talk of the devil,' he said.

'There she is herself. The young lady that I've been telling you about.'

'Well then, young lady, and what can I do for you?' the butcher asked.

I was a bit uncertain about this 'young lady' thing. The only times that I had been called young lady before were the times when I was in someone's bad books. 'Could you oblige me with some scraps for my dog please, butcher?'

'A big dog?' he asked.

I hesitated, then said, 'A collie, sir.'

He went to the back shop and returned in minutes with a big parcel which he put into an onion bag. 'There you are,' he said. 'No, no. No charge,' refusing my sixpence. 'Not if it's for a collie.'

I handed Tommy the sixpence worth of mixed sweets which was quite a lot in those days. 'You'll have to share them,' I told him.

He considered this remark below an answer. So he just gave me a look, which had it been a blow, would have felled an oak.

20

We could hear the souch of the camp long before we reached it. The weans were merry now that their folks had sobered up, and were louping about at play. Some of the men were playing quoits amidst much talk and laughter. Some of the women who were not in the horrors of drink had gone to take some houses, in the hope of getting bread or something for the bairns to eat. Ricky ran to meet me, like I had been gone for weeks.

Uncle Jimmie blessed me a thousand times for some of the tobacco, but refused the money. He did, however, examine his bagpipes. They were his only earthly treasure—of course I mean things, not people. Mother too clamoured for the tobacco. She looked much better now after a wash and having combed her long hair. She shared her tobacco with the women, and Uncle Jimmie shared with the men. Soon there were a lot of contented-looking faces with smoke blowing from their mouths. Mother was amazed at the amount of money in Tommy's bonnet. It too was shared, and spent on food.

When I went to feed Ricky, I discovered that the butcher had included about two pounds of lovely lean steak along with Ricky's scraps. People are strange, I thought. I had deliberately been bad. Full of venom and defiance, and had received undreamt-of rewards for it. Had I remained quietly shy and retiring like I was wont to do, most of the time, I am sure that less than a quarter of the money would have been in that wee bonnet. No steak, a rare treat for us, would have been in that parcel either.

The rest of that day I spent walking with Annie and her dead sister's baby. Grief does not really linger too long with the very young. She was quite bright and the best of company.

The baby's father too had his brighter moments. Aunt Martha and Uncle Geordie, however, would be long and long before they could get their spirits lifted. When I had said 'How are you?' during the bout of drinking, Uncle Geordie had replied, 'If we drank the contents of a distillery, it would neither make us drunk nor deaden the pangs of losing Elsie.'

That night nature decided to chastise her clouds, and their mighty roars and sair weeping awoke me in the small hours of the morning. The angry tears had no difficulty penetrating our makeshift tent, which had been hurriedly erected and made up of bits and pieces of old covers, mostly cotton.

It was still dark, but I could smell Mother's pipe and knew that she was lying smoking. 'Ma, my head is drookit with drips,' I whispered, because I didn't want to wake Lexy who was afraid of thunder and lightning.

'Aye,' she answered. 'Don't touch the tent for God's sake or we'll all be drowned. Lie down and hap your head.'

Of course Mother was not really afraid that we would drown. Travelling people nearly always exaggerate very much. For instance they might say, "I met Sandy Cameron today and he had a bundle bigger than Ben Nevis on his back." Or "There is tons of sugar in my basket there." It is just their way of speaking.

While I am on the subject of speaking, perhaps I should let you know that if I were to write in the way that travellers speak to each other, you would understand very little of what I wrote. So I have decided to use very little of the traveller's cant.

Anyway, we all had to get up that night. Uncle Jimmie had a very large pure tarpaulin tent, and we all had to huddle inside it. The boys had dug a trench around it, cursing as the rain drenched them. The trench was to run the water away from the tent and prevent underwater. The women had taken the driest of their bedding to keep the wee ones warm. 'God hae mercy on us aa,' Mother said. 'The world's at an end wi' the power of rain.'

Came daylight and still it rained. 'I could dae wi' a mouthful o' tea,' Aunt Martha said. She had her tartan plaid around her and the baby was sleeping snugly in her bosom under it.

'We could never get a fire going. It's like a burn all round about us, Ma.' Willie was wringing the sleeves of his jacket as he spoke.

'I'm going to try and get a drop tea made,' Jean ventured. 'Who's coming with me?'

'Me!' I shouted. I had a huge golf umbrella which I had rescued from amongst rubbish thrown out for the scaffies, and I was eager to try it out. We stepped out of the tent and up to the knees in water.

'I'll get my big kettle,' Jean said and as we waded towards her tent a wooden kist, which she used when packing, floated past us.

Jean saluted it, singing *Speed Bonny Boat*. I thought this very funny and couldn't help laughing. I got my umbrella and mother's big black tea can, also Uncle Jimmie's. Jean took two large iron kettles, and a tin with tea in it.

As we waded towards the road Jean burst out laughing. 'We are wise folk!' she laughed. 'Up to the knees in water and with a monster umbrella above our head. Oh yes, we are truly wise.' I knew where we were making for, the smiddy, which was quite near, beside the wee burn. That morning it was running red in spate. However the smith was very sympathetic. He knew Jean and as there was a tap at the door he offered to fill the cans and kettles. Then he put them on to boil, telling us to dry ourselves. It was cosy in the smiddy, and when the smith asked, 'Are ye washed oot up at the quarry?' I answered, 'Aye, it's flooded.' Jean cleared her throat—a warning and flashed me a look which said 'Shut up!'

I had spoken without thinking. Now I realised that Jean was terrified that the smith would send 'the Cruelty' up to see if the children were suffering.

'Are the bairns alright, Jean?' were the smith's very next words.

'Oh aye. They are all as healthy as wee troots,' Jean answered. It's just that we couldn't get a fire lighted. The sticks are too wet, but it's fine and dry inside the tents.' Jean put some tea into the kettles and cans which soon came to the boil.

'Can I leave this umbrella here?' I asked the smith. 'I can't manage it and the tea cans.'

'Aye, surely, lass. It will be safe enough here.'

The rain had abated a bit as we hurried back to the quarry. 'God forgie me, but you have to tell them lies,' Jean said. 'If a Cruelty did come now, all the weans would be whipped away.'

Running with full cans was no problem to us, as we were so used to carrying buckets of water. Neither of us spilt a drop of the tea, but we did splash ourselves soaken with water.

'God bless you, daughters,' Aunt Martha greeted us. She had the tea dishes all ready.

'Ah, that's better,' Hendry said after his bowl of tea. 'I'll awa' noo and try to start the old van. I must get dry straw for the beds tonight.'

'Come here, lassie,' Mother cried to me, from the rear of the tent. 'Look what Aunt Martha is giving you.' She was holding out a lovely sun-ray skirt and a green jersey. 'Here,'

52

she continued, handing me her plaid, 'put them on before
you get your blue death.'

Jean was already wriggling under a plaid, getting into
something dry. The skirt and jersey fitted and I thanked
Aunt Martha when I came out from under the plaid.

21

A watery sun timidly peeped through the clouds about mid-
day. Then sent them scoorin, from her sight, so that her
welcome rays spread joy all over us. Annie had been sitting
as if asleep with her back against the rear tentpole, and a
cover drawn up over her. For hours she had sat there without
speaking. All the others were outside now, to get their share of
the sun. So I went in and sat down beside her. 'I got these from
your mother,' I began, pointing to the clothes I had on.

'I told her to give them to you,' she answered. 'They are
too small for me.'

'Are you feeling things a bit today, Annie?' I asked.

Tears immediately filled her eyes and taking her hand out
from under the cover she opened it and held out a gold earring.
'I found that when I was climbing over the dyke up there last
night. I saw something shining and when I lifted it up I nearly
fainted.' It was Elsie's earring.

'Suddenly I remembered how I had envied her those earrings, how I had gone off the fang with Mother for giving
them to her instead of me.' Annie was sobbing pitifully now.
'Oh, Betsy, I feel terrible. When Elsie lost this one she said
to me, "No better thing could happen to me. I should have
given you the earrings, Annie. You put your eye on them,
didn't you?" Oh God, if I had only known.'

I put my arms around her, saying, 'Annie, you shouldn't
feel so bad. Everyone has regrets when they lose a loved
one. I went through hell when Daddy died. Then I realised that Daddy loved me, and understood. Believe me, I
done things a thousand times worse than envying a pair

of earrings. That was nothing. Come on out. The sun is shining.'

All the grown-ups were very active. Every bush had a blanket, sheet, or bed-cover spread over it, steaming in the sun. The bedding straw had all been raked in a heap to be burned. Camp-sticks were being pulled out and re-erected on less trodden ground. Mother and my aunts were away shopping.

The water had been directed by little ditches into one main ditch to carry it away. The wee ones were having great fun watching their little boats, mostly pieces of wood, float down the ditches. Hendry returned with his van packed full of bunches of straw and two huge bags of gaswork cinders, and then made a brazier out of an old oil drum.

Jeanie had fed the two babies, and had not as yet eaten herself. Soon Mother and my aunts returned from the town, and they were laden. They had been scranning the shops for anything that was going: cuttings of bacon from the ham machine, bread and buns from the day before, scraps of meat from the butcher's, fruit just on the turn, hard cheese, and even tobacco which had gone hard and dry. Those things only cost them a few pennies.

The men had gathered firewood and a big fire was lit as well as the brazier. Pots were soon put on and everyone fed—children first, then the men, and lastly the women.

Ricky shared Hendry's van at night with four other dogs, greyhounds, two bantam hens and a bantam cock. The bantams belonged to young Tommy. Now they were all capering about in the mud and wet. Ricky had one bad habit. He liked to share whatever we were eating as well as his own, and got quite annoyed if we didn't let him taste everything. He was timid to cowardice with the other dogs, but they never took advantage of this.

The ponies were shifted to better grazing ground. Now all that was wanting was a cover for our tent. 'I'll go round some of the farms, Aunt Maggie, and see if I can pick up an old cover for you,' Hendry told Mother. 'I might pick up a puckle scrap or something while I'm at it.' Katie and

Nellie went with him for a run. The other men decided to go for a chase with the dogs. They took Ricky with them although he could never catch a hare.

So the only man left at the camp was Peter, the young bereaved husband. He was sitting near the fire nursing his baby, crooning to it softly. His mother, a dark industrious wee woman, was standing gazing at him and the baby very tenderly. She was nicknamed Toosh, because there were so many Marys around.

I had helped Annie to make her family's beds with the fresh straw. 'Feeling better now, Annie?' I had asked.

'A wee bit,' she had answered, 'but what should I do about the earring? Mother has the other one in a little box.'

'You should tell her, Annie.'

'But I don't want to hurt her any more.'

'Tell her,' I urged.

Now as we all gathered around the huge fire, the older women sitting on old oil drums or whatever, Annie decided to take my advice. 'Ma,' she started, 'I have found something.'

'Aye, what is it?' her mother asked. 'A five pound note, I hope. I could do wi' a new pipe. This one has seen better days.' Aunt Martha held up her very blackened clay pipe.

'Look, Ma,' said Annie, holding out her open hand with the earring in it.

Aunt Martha sagged and paled. 'Elsie's earring,' she whispered. The jocular note had disappeared from her voice. 'We searched long and sair for that earring.'

Elsie's husband put in, 'I'm sure we turned every blade of grass for miles around the camp. She wanted to give them to you, Annie. She said that you liked them.' He stood up as he spoke and gave the baby to Mother. 'Hold a minute, Maggie. I must put on more sticks,' he said, turning away, but not before we saw the tears fill his eyes.

Annie threw herself down at her mother's feet and put her head on her lap. 'Oh Mammie, Mammie,' she cried, sobbing. 'I wish I hadn't begrudged her the earrings. I should have died, not Elsie.'

On and on Annie went, sobbing out the words which were

55

giving her heart so much pain. 'Wheesht, wean,' her mother told her, stroking her hair, 'dinnae think like that. You have little need to have a sorry heart about your sister. You were closer than twins. I wish that the weight on my heart was no heavier than that. It's just a wee lesson that we aa have to learn the hard way.'

She then looked up at all of us standing round the fire and continued. 'Now aa you lassies standing here. Tak' tent o' this and never, ever, covet anything. Nor envy anyone. A wee bit o' jealousy between a lad and lass, or between man and wife, is excusable. Dinnae ever envy or covet things.'

I am sure that the hearts of all of us around that fire burst wide, then closed again with Aunt Martha's words inside them. Mine certainly did.

'Do you want to keep the earrings, Annie?' Aunt Martha asked.

'No, no, Ma. Maybe I should, to remind me of this day, but I couldn't bear a constant reminder.' Annie had stopped crying, but she still trembled.

'What about you, Betsy?' Aunt Martha held out the earrings towards me.

I backed away, shaking my head.

'You, Jean?'—but Jean too refused her offer, and so did all the women and girls around the fire.

Peter had joined us again. 'Burn them, Martha,' he told her. So those beautiful eighteen-carat gold earrings, set with precious rubies, emeralds and seed pearls, were thrown into the brazier which burned in front of Hendry and Jean's tent.

'They will never cause another tear to be shed,' Aunt Martha whispered.

Idiocy, you might say. Travelling people, however, thought that things could hold unseen powers of good or evil. Unsanctified things—things with the spirit of evil—were dreaded and burned, buried, or thrown away.

In Annie's case it was more because Elsie was a cold corpse. How could Annie possibly enjoy wearing those earrings? If Elsie had given them to her, then they would have been cherished. The rest of us thought that they just might be unsanctified. Then why not sell them, you might ask. Well, the money gotten for them would have been considered unsanctified too. Blood money.

22

Anyway, Hendry did pick up two old stack-covers for our tent and also had bought two or three hundredweights of brock wool from the same farmer. Wool was a good price then, and the brock, which was mostly belly clippings and rear clippings, were knotted with the sheep's droppings. Wool buyers would not handle it. So the traveller men bought it very cheaply. 'That will be a job for you lassies the morn,' Hendry said, 'cleaning that wool for me.'

We all slept soundly that night, and next morning whilst the older women were away taking the houses, as peddling was called, we younger ones started to clean Hendry's wool. With old scissors we clipped any clean wool away from the dirt. Hendry would get half-a-crown for every pound of clean wool. So although this was a nauseating, stinking job, it was worth the trouble.

Still we were all glad to see the end of it. When we all walked to a wee burn to wash, several of us discovered sheep's ticks bored into our flesh with only their tail ends sticking out. So amidst skirling and screeching and more than a few oaths, we stripped our clothes off. 'Is there any on my back?' Katie was shouting.

'Oh, I'm sure there is one in my oxter.' This from Nellie.

'I'm sure they are in among my hair too,' Jean, always the comedian, shouted, 'and not the hair of my head, or my oxters!' Then more loudly she cried, 'I see two men coming.' Her laughter rippled cheerily as we scurried for the cover of bushes and long grass.

'God pity you, Jean,' Annie said as she emerged with a badly scratched shoulder.

'Did I tell you tae dive into a bramble bush?' Jean laughed.

On this Nellie, Katie and Annie dived on her, holding her down in the water. Her fierce struggling and shouting of 'Gadgie! Shaness! Shaness!' were ignored, until one of them glanced up and sure enough an elderly gamekeeper stood on the bank, his dog at his feet. My other cousins and I, although partly dressed, had seen him coming and were now well hidden on the opposite bank of the burn. Peeping out, we saw their mad scramble for the bushes.

The jolly-looking gamekeeper's eyes bulged in his head. 'Man, we've come the right airt the day, Rover,' he was telling his dog. 'I niver believed in water babies afore. It just goes tae show ye, min.' Most of our clothes were lying around his feet. Rover was having a wee sniff at them. 'Aweel, they've disappeared. I maun away hame and tell Kirsty aboot this. She'll niver believe me.' Of course he was talking for our benefit.

When he was out of sight much giggling and shouts of 'Shaness!, Shaness!' filled the air. We joked, giggled, and laughed until we were near the tents. Then we all became strangely quiet.

Mother eyed us for a few minutes. She and Aunt Martha were just home a few minutes before us. The women usually went to the houses in pairs. Lexy had been with her. 'You are a real cheery-looking bunch,' Mother said.

Then a babble of voices began to relate our ploy, amidst much laughter. 'I've ran oot o' laughter,' Jean said. 'My sides are sair.'

'You had better mak' sure that there is nane o' they ticks aboot you, Jean,' Mother told her. 'If one should get on to the young wean. . . .' She left the rest to our imagination.

'For God's sake dinnae tell Hendry!' Jean of course meant about the gamekeeper seeing them naked.

'Maybe they won't tell him, but I will.' It was Willie's voice. He had been sitting making a basket behind the tent, and none of us had noticed him. He came striding round as he spoke. Looking directly at me he said, 'I suppose he seen you naked too.' From the look in his eyes I knew better than to cross him, so I with difficulty held my tongue. 'You are nothing but a bunch of barming mares,' he went on, before striding away with a face like thunder.

23

After supper Annie and I went walking. A path ran along the edge of the fields above the quarry. In those days there were many paths and many walkers. Everything had dried up well after the cloudburst, but the fields were a sorry sight. The tassels of corn which had been dancing in the sun were lying forlornly on the earth. The bearded barley, too, had taken a hammering. The wheat which three days ago had stood higher than me, was thrown down like a golden carpet across the fields. This made me really vexed. Why say *Mother Nature*? I thought. This was more the act of a stepmother, and a very cruel stepmother at that. Or was there in nature, as in humans, a struggle between the forces of good and evil.

My thoughts were interrupted by Annie. 'Did you see Willie's face when he thought that the keeper had seen you naked?' she was saying. 'He was boiling,' she went on. 'He is surely really determined to make you his wife.'

How could I answer her? He was her brother. So I asked her if she had a lad, as we were wont to say. That did the trick. She began to tell me about a half-cousin of hers who lived in Argyllshire and I let her talk. I was very fond of Annie, yet I knew that the least hint of anything against her brother would end our friendship.

We returned about seven o'clock. 'It's about time you were here to do some work,' Katie greeted me. She had been left to wash the dishes and pots. 'I'm needin' water to wash with,' she went on.

'What's wrong wi' the burn?' I asked her.

'I want hot water,' she said.

'Well I doubt you will want it,' I answered, 'except you fetch it yourself.'

'Come, come, wee woman,' Mother put in. 'You have had plenty of scouth all day. Fetch the water for your sister.'

Actually I would have been very pleased to go for two pails of water, or many more, if I could have gotten away by myself. It seemed that I had never been alone since we left the house. Travellers always did almost everything together. Men, women, girls, and children were rarely alone. I, however, really needed a little solitude. I got very irritable and just couldn't seem to function properly without it. Just as I thought, two girls ran after me as I walked away with the buckets. Four children, too, came along. I took care not to show them how I felt, knowing that the fault was in myself, if fault it was.

24

The flattened harvest fields pleased my uncles, because the farmers would need plenty of help, and they would be sure to get work for their families. They found a farmer who needed them, near Dull. So two days later we were on our way there. Hendry took the older women and young children in his van. Jean was asked to go with them to feed the wee infant, but refused. The back and front of the van was already packed.

'Then I will have to walk too?' Aunt Martha queried.

'Nae need,' Jean told her. 'I will carry the two weans. They will be like roasted kippers sitting in that van. I would rather walk.' The bantams were in a wee coop tied to one of the carts.

We walked along behind the carts, taking turns at carrying the infant and Jean's baby. Some of the boys had bicycles. We must have made a strange sight as we went along, but nobody gave us a second glance. People were used to seeing travellers on the move and paid no more attention than they would to a bull in a field.

We stopped beside a wee burn to make tea and to let Jean feed the weans. Her own baby was five months old now and was beginning to eat a little. So she chewed some food and popped it from her mouth into his. Disgusting, you may think, but traveller women did this often. Nyams, they called it. It never seemed to do the weans any harm.

Schiehallion stood quite near to the moor where we were to camp, and there would be no shortage of firewood. We chose a place near a wee burn, some distance from the farm. There was a lot of wooded area. Just ideal for us. We had carried our camp sticks with us, which was just as well as we could see no hazel saplings here.

The rest of the day was spent getting everything in order. We were to start cutting and binding and stooking a twenty-three-acre field of corn, which was completely flattened. Scythes were provided by the farmer, and only the men used them. We started and finished when we felt like it. There was no set time for anything and we got paid by the acre.

There was plenty of scouth for the weans, and all of us younger ones sang, joked, laughed and frolicked as we worked. If it became very warm during the day, we all stopped work. The older ones would sit under trees cracking and smoking and drinking tea. Uncle Jimmie would have the young pipers in the company sitting in a ring, with him in the middle, teaching them to play in the evening. Some girls, too joined him. Since hearing me play, they too wanted to learn.

25

One evening Peter took an old melodeon out of its box and began to play it. When he started to play *Flora McDonald's Lament*, Jean started to sing it. This had been his wife Elsie's favourite song. I looked up from where I was sitting on a tree stump at Annie. She dropped her eyes to the ground, then with a deep sigh raised them again and began to sing along with Jean.

Mother, who had been resting in the tent, came out and scanned us all. Aunt Martha and Uncle Geordie too had emerged and were walking slowing towards us. Mother opened her mouth to reprehend the singers, but Aunt Martha stopped her. 'Leave them, Maggie,' she said. 'I am pleased that they feel able to sing the song,' and she too joined in the last verse. We could see that she was fighting tears, yet she bravely smiled when the song ended.

Uncle Geordie, who had been standing with his eyes on the ground, lifted them and said, 'What's thon ither wee sang that she used tae sing? Sing thon yin.'

'*The Ill Getted Loon?*' Peter asked.

'No, no' that yin. The wee sang aboot Bonny Glenshee.' Uncle Geordie turned to Katie. 'You sing it, Katie,' he said.

So Katie sang *The Glenshee Lullaby* while Peter played it.

'Noo what aboot yin o' Sandy's sangs? God rest him, and may his bed be in Heaven.' Aunt Martha turned and looked at Mother as she spoke.

'That was yin o' his favourites which Katie sang,' Mother told her. 'He was affie fond o' Glenshee. His folk used tae camp up there when he was young. I'll sing ye a wee sang that I heard *his* mother sing. If I can mind on it.'

O hie, bonny lassie, come ower the burn
And if yer sheep wander I will gie them a turn
Sae happy I'd be, lass, beneath yon green shade.
Gin ye wad come wi' me and sit in my plaid.

I hae a wee doggie that trots at my heel
And this little doggie I loo' it sae weel
I'd gie't tae ye lassie and mair gin I haed
Gin ye wad come wi' me and sit in my plaid.

I hae a wee whittle it's made o' true steel
And this little whittle I loo it sae weel
I'd gie't tae ye Annie and mair gin I haed
Gin ye wad come wi' me and sit in my plaid.

Twa yowes and a lambie are aa that I've got
But I'd tak' the wee lambie fae this little flock
And gie't tae ye lassie, and mair gin I haed
If ye wad come wi' me and sit in my plaid.

Mother stopped there, saying, 'I dinnae ken if that's aa she sang or no'. It's aa that I heard her sing. She was a Reid, and

was as bonny a wumen as ever travelled Perthshire. She had
bottle-black hair, curly like a watter dug. Everybody ca'd her
Bonnie Maggie.' Mother was speaking for the benefit of us
younger ones who couldn't remember Granny or had never
seen her.

The days were shortening and darkness was creeping in.
Uncle Jimmie brought us back to earth by exclaiming loudly,
'Hey, you young women, get they weans intae their beds, and
get a drop tea made. Is there water in for morning? Laddies,
come on, jump! We'll need mair sticks than that. Did the
horses get a drink?'

We hastened to do Uncle Jimmie's bidding.

26

We were there for nearly a month, and during that time only
the married ones had been into a town or village. When the
young men were not working they wandered with their dogs,
sometimes climbing a bit up the mountain. Annie and I always
went to the farm for the milk, in the early evening. We always
stopped to speak to a very old man who sat on a seat at the side
of the old road. He lived with his son who was the cattle-man.
He looked so lonely there all by himself. So we left the camp
early to give him half an hour or so of our company. He was
an Aberdeenshire man and we loved to listen to his native
tongue as he told us tales of his youth.

This particular evening he was making tappies for the top
of the stacks. He was very skilled at this, making all kinds
of different shapes. He had taught us how to make a thistle,
one of the simplest shapes.

He was making a shape of two horses, a plough, and even
the man behind the plough. He used no more than a bit wire
along with the grain that he made them from.

'Fin I was a loon, we used til mak' a floorie wi' corn an
wear it on oor breests. Syne we wid gang tae the mairt. This
is fit we did if we were needin' a hairst. If the fairmer saw ye

63

wi' this in yer buttonhole, he kent you were wantin' a job at the hairst. Syne ye made a bargain wi' him, maybe for four or five poun'. If the hairst lasted a fortnight, ye got what ye had bargained for, an' if it lasted sax weeks ye just got the same. Ye had tae stick tae yer bargain.'

We sat close to him watching the old feeble fingers, expertly twist the wheat, corn and wire.

'Well, we are away for the milk. See you on our way back,' Annie said as we rose to go.

'Haud on a meenit, queens, I hae something tae tell ye,' he said.

'Something good?' I asked him.

'Well, I'm nae sae share aboot that. It's like this, ye see. Oh I ken ye are twa bonny eneuch lasses, but I'm no' needin' an umman body.'

I watched Annie's eyes and mouth open to double their size. 'What did he say?' she quickly asked in cant.

'He's no needin' an umman body, Annie,' I told her.

Her laughter was almost screamed out.

'My son's wife is guid tae me, and I dinna think they wad be pleased if I ta'en an umman. Onywye, I'm gettin' ower auld.' Old Charlie then held up the tappie which he had made. It was truly a work of art.

Annie regained her grip on herself and asked him, 'Would ye have picked me, Charlie? You would have, wouldn't ye?'

'Noo I'm no gaen tae say,' he answered.

I could hold my laughter no longer. So I took off with Annie at my heels until we were out of his earshot. Then, throwing ourselves down on the ground, we rolled about until we were weak with the power of laughter. 'I'm no needin' an umman body,' Annie kept repeating, between our bursts of giggles.

27

'Come on, Annie. The milk!' We rose and made our way towards the farm, still laughing, and went into the byre.

Ella the maid was milking. 'You twa are affa happy the night. Dinnae tell me. I ken. You have gotten a lad.' This re-started our laughter, especially when we thought about the lad. Ella was a bit hallie-wracket, but a very good worker. 'I aince had a lad,' she said, 'I used to chap at the bothy window, and get chasies. One night one of the lads chased me right round to the barn.'

'I'll bet you enjoyed that,' I said. Then the three of us howled with laughter.

Then who should come stepping into the byre but the farmer's wife. 'What's going on in here? What's aa the racket about?'

Ella jumped and became immediately humble. 'Sorry, madam,' she said.

'Get on with your work. You have little to giggle about,' the farmer's wife continued.

'Yes, maam, no, maam, sorry, maam.' Ella was all upset.

The woman then turned to Annie and me, saying, 'As for you two, I just can't understand you. You don't even have a roof over your heads. No security. Nothing. Yet you would think that you hadn't a care in the world.'

'Begging your pardon, Mrs McPherson, but we happen to have the very best security that can be found in this world.' I watched Annie as she spoke, and knew that she was angry.

'I can't see where this security is,' Mrs McPherson answered. 'Our trust in our Maker, that is our security.'

'And what would you folk ken about your Maker?' The woman stared at us as she spoke.

'Very little,' Annie answered her. 'No more than I do about the air that we breathe, but I ken that we need them both just to live.'

'Well spoken, lass. I've just fallen out with the farmer and I'm taking it out on you girls. He has gone and invited six farmers to come and see a patch of wheat that has been treated with some new-fangled stuff. He has watched it growing as if it was a bairn. Of course he's also asked them to stay for dinner. The bloody nerve of that man! Excuse me swearing, girls. He kens that I have more than enough to do tomorrow.

Ella is a good help but, God Almighty, we're not broonies. I'd like to see him do half as much work as we put in. Hearing you three laughing was just ower much for me.'

'We can understand that, Mrs McPherson,' I told her. I really felt for her, knowing that all the unmarried ploughmen were fed in the farmhouse. Also that she and Ella made cheese and butter, and gathered eggs and prepared fowls for the local shops.

Suddenly she said, 'Hey! I've got an idea. Would you two girls like to come tomorrow evening and give us a hand? I have blacks you could wear.'

'Oh! Missus,' I let out, 'I hardly ken a spoon from a ladle.'

'Ach, away with you,' she answered. 'You will come, won't you, round about six tomorrow night?'

When I saw Annie nod I followed suit, but was more than a little apprehensive.

'That's a queer time o' night to have dinner,' I said to Annie as we made our way home with the milk.

'Nearly all they toff kind o' folk have dinner at night,' she told me.

28

So next day Annie and I left the cornfield early. We had washed our cotton dresses the night before, leaving them hanging out all night to free them from wrinkles. Our undies had to be hung on a little rope strung across the inside of our tents, lest they offended the eyes of the men. On no account could girls' or women's underwear, even if new, be left anywhere where male eyes could see them. We used to fold whatever clothes we possessed into a pillow-case, and use them as a pillow. If we needed a clean blouse or whatever, we would hang it out all night. The night air was as good as ironing.

After bathing and washing our hair in a secluded part of

the wee burn, we dressed and made ourselves as presentable as possible.

On our way to the farm, we talked about Ella the servant girl. 'I can see my father giving her a kick on the shuch one of these nights,' Annie was saying. Ella had been coming to the camp on her time off and when she finished in the evenings. There she would sit at the fire on an orange box, with her legs wide apart and her dress above her knees. The men always walked away, some of the young ones with red faces.

On her last visit she had shouted to Uncle Geordie, Annie's father, 'Hoo the hell do aa you men leave the fireside when I come?'

'Listen, hussy,' he had answered her, 'you sit there making sheepy eyes at the laddies, with your claes very near above your head. Do you see any o' our lassies or women doing that? Keep your legs together, lassie, and pull down your claes. There's naebody here wants to see your sporran.'

'You daft auld hairy. You're naething but a fool. You cannae see anything but my underwear, and they are clean and well paid for.'

'Well paid for I can believe, missie, but I'm not sure about clean. Nae clean lassie would sit like that.' Uncle Geordie was livid with anger, but Ella was quite undaunted.

'Away you go, you haverin' auld ass,' she told him.

He did go, muttering his wrath in cant and threatening all the women and girls with dire consequences if we didn't get rid of her, and quick.

If any traveller woman had spoken to him in like manner, there is no doubt that he would have kicked her on the shuch. When travelling people think of cleanliness, they don't think as non-travellers. To them dirt was anything that issued from the human body. A really dirty man or woman was an unchaste one. The earth was not regarded as dirt. Everything that is eaten sprang from the earth. So how could it be dirty? Uncleanliness in personal hygiene could cause many vile diseases, they thought. At that time no traveller woman would eat from the hands of a man, because he had to handle himself when doing the toilet.

Even the men themselves, when out working in the fields, would pick up a slice of bread by the crust and eat all but the piece touched by their fingers. This they threw away. Women did the same. Many old travellers still have this habit. They will throw away the last piece of anything they are eating from their hand, just through force of habit. More often than not, a burn or even ditch-water could be found to wash the hands in. Married people must always wash their hands before touching food or dishes in the morning.

29

However, let's get back to the farmhouse which Annie and I had arrived at earlier than requested. The farmer's wife gave us black dresses and white aprons to put on, then fixed little white lace caps on our heads. Ella was busy preparing vegetables as if the future of mankind depended on her speed, rattling and clattering dishes and oven doors all the while. Forgetting her place in her excitement, she was even ordering and dictating to Mrs McPherson. The good lady just smiled her exasperation, and shook her head.

'We will set the table for you,' Annie volunteered, lifting the silver which was laid out on a clean napkin. 'Come and help, Betsy.' We went into the dining room where a large oval table was covered with a damask cover. 'Look,' Annie answered my bewildered stare. 'It's really easy. See the way I am putting these. Here, you can surely do that, while I get the glasses and other things.

'That's fine,' she continued, when she returned. 'Mrs McPherson can't get awa' from something she is browning in front of the fire.'

I tried to help Annie as best I could, and when the farmer's wife did come ben shortly afterwards, she gave an exclamation of pleased surprise. 'Don't thank me,' I told her. 'Annie is the one who is doing almost everything.'

'You have done this type of thing before, Annie?' Mrs McPherson asked.

'Aye, I worked in a big hotel in Pitlochry for four months last winter.'

This was news to me. I wondered why she had never mentioned it.

'I was getting on fine,' Annie continued, 'until someone told the proprietor that I was a traveller. I'm still smarting a bit from the tongueing that his wife gave me. "The sheer audacity of you!" she shouted, almost screamed, at me. "A tinker under my roof, serving my guests! If people find out, I might as well close down." This is the way that woman went on. I never felt so low in my life.'

I could see from Annie's face how deeply hurt she had been.

'That is unforgivable,' the farmer's wife said. 'Don't let it bother you, child. Heavens! The men are coming. Don't get nervous, Betsy.'

Mrs McPherson had killed a young grumfie and two fat hens, and although she had no gas or electricity they were now roasted to perfection. The top of the big shining black range was covered with pots, pans, and roasting tins. Annie served, the farmer's wife dished up, and I removed the dishes, taking them through to Ella, who washed them. There were lots of silver dishes and large tureens which Mrs McPherson would not let Ella wash. 'I will do them for you,' Annie told Mrs McPherson. 'You can join the men now.' The farmers were now sitting in the parlour with glasses of malt whisky in front of them.

I helped Annie to do the silver. Ella soon made short work of all the pots and pans. After Annie and I had changed back into our own clothes, we had meant to slip out the back door and go home. The farmer's wife, however, came through before we could. 'Come,' she said. 'The farmers want to meet you.' Annie and I followed her through to the parlour, where a second bottle of whisky was just being opened. 'This is Betsy and Annie, who kindly came to help out tonight. They are living on the moor. Their families are cutting that cornfield which was flattened. The girls are just leaving now.'

I scanned the faces of the men through lowered eyelashes. There were expressions of surprise, of unbelief, and even shock, but none of displeasure. In fact they nearly all smiled kindly.

One very tall man stood up and took two half-crowns out of his trouser pocket. 'You done very well, girls,' he said. The others all followed suit. We shook our heads when offered the money, but Mrs McPherson put it into our hands.

We left the farmhouse with nearly a pound each, and a basket of left-overs. 'That is more than we could earn in a week working,' Annie said. 'I never thought that she would tell them that we are nakens. She is really very nice.'

We both felt very good at being treated so nicely and getting praised for our work. To add to our pleasure the gloaming was beautifying the earth. Have you ever noticed how lovely everything becomes in the gloaming? Even people. Annie, a bonny lassie at any time, was a picture of fair sweetness in its flattering light. The scent of wild mint and ferns added to my bliss. I breathed in deeply.

30

I really felt good, but it was not to last long. As we turned round a bend in the path who should be coming to meet us but Peter and Willie. Oh hell! I thought. I hope he doesn't start his di-does. He had been getting more and more persistent. Of course I mean Willie.

I knew that some of the men would come to meet us. Traveller men always do when darkness is falling. Annie ran excitedly to meet them, showing them the money and telling them all about what we had seen and been doing in the farmhouse.

'Your tongue is like the clattering bone o' a duck's backside, lassie,' Peter chided, but he used another word for backside.

'All right,' Annie told him, 'for that you don't get one haet oot o' the basket.' She lifted the linen tea-cloth which covered the contents of the basket as she spoke. Then she darted away from him, and he took after her.

I was about to run after them, but Willie caught my arm. 'Wait a minute. I want to speak to you,' he said. 'I heard your mother say that she is going home to the house soon.'

'Aye, Lexy has to go back to school,' I answered.

'What about you?' he asked. 'Are you going too?'

'Of course I am,' I told him.

'I am more than fond of you, Betsy. We would be great together. You playing your pipes to the gentry and me playing mine, all summer. We could get a car. Why don't we run away right now?' He was holding my shoulders as he spoke.

'No, Willie,' I said loudly, pulling away from him.

'No? No? Is that aa you can say, lassie? Always no?'

'I'm not ready for that,' I told him.

'Not ready?' He was shouting now, 'You just don't want to, do you?'

'That's right. I don't want to!' I was getting angry now.

'You are an aggravating, provoking lassie. I have a good mind to. . . .' He stopped talking and grabbed me fiercely.

'You just stop that, Willie. You know that I have no brothers nor even a father, but I have plenty cousins on my father's side. They will soon sort you out.'

He then let me go, saying, 'I could wipe my backside with the best cousin that you have on your father's side.'

'Ho, laddie,' I answered, 'you would have to ripe aa your pockets for the ability to do thon.'

'Lassie, I'll get hung for you!' He picked up a thick stick as ye spoke.

For a minute I thought that he meant to carry out his threat, but he took his spite out on the undergrowth instead, laying on to the grass, bracken, ferns and bushes as he walked along. When he took a swipe at a baby rabbit which ran across the path, I bolted and soon caught up with Peter and Annie.

'Where's Willie?' she asked.

'Coming,' I told her, which he did within a few minutes, his anger spent. He was now sullen and morose.

Ricky was overjoyed at my return, springing up into my arms and attempting to lick my neck. 'I couldnae tak' ye,' I told him. 'Down ye go, you wee spoiled creature.' I bent down, fondling and talking to Ricky to avoid letting Mother look at me and see my agitated spirit. My mother, however, had uncanny powers of observation and knew that I was disturbed. Well too did she ken the reason.

She walked away over to our tent, then called on me. 'Betsy, come and trim the wick o' this lamp. I can't see to do a thing. I'll have to look for a pair o' specs to mysel'.

'Has that laddie been bothering you again?' she asked, when I entered the tent. We were out of earshot of the others here.

'Oh, Ma,' I answered, 'I want to go home. He even killed a tiny wee rabbit. He was just a lump of pure venom.' I was trying to suppress sobs now. 'He fears me, Ma.'

'I ken, wean. We'll gang hame on Friday. Here, hae a wee draw o' my pipe. I'll see to it that he winnae get you on your own again. His mother has that laddie ruined. He has never been refused onything that was within her power to give him. Come, we will go out to the fire now and see what they are all doing.'

31

Willie, however, burned his boats the following night. Ella came along at around the back of six o'clock. 'I'm gaen tae be a good lassie the night, and keep my claes doon. So aa you mannies neednae rin away,' she said.

'You had better watch your tongue tae,' Uncle Jimmie told her. 'We want nae crack aboot wimmen's wye o' doing either.'

'You're a right daft auld bugger. Awa' and boil yer heid,' she answered him.

He did gang away, with his blood boiling, if not his head.

Annie went for a long, heavy rope which we used for skipping. 'Come on, Ella, for a game.' Going a good length away from the fire we commenced to skip with double ropes. All the girls and young women, married ones as well, joined in. Jean cut the heels from Ella more than once when she cawed the rope, causing Ella to fall. 'You bugger, Jean. I'll mak' you pee a hedgehog if I get a haud o' you.' Ella took all our ribbing in good part, and many a laugh we had at her antics.

We played there till Toosh shouted to us to come for tea. We always had tea around eight o'clock. 'Come lassies, it's gloamin' dark, and ye'll no' see what you are putting in your mouths shortly.'

Ella came with us, and placed herself down on an upturned orange box, beside the fire, and pulled her wide skirt down to her ankles. 'Surely that will please you lot,' she said, looking up at the men. 'Oh hey! is that oatcake you are makin'? Gie's a daed o' it! It smells fine,' she went on.

'Hurry up and eat it then,' Toosh told her. 'It's time that you were makin' your way hame. It will be dark in a minute.'

Mother and Aunt Martha had been away up the wee burn for water, and Mother laid her pail of water down to rest her arm and to talk a wee. I told Ella that Annie and I would walk a bit of the road home with her. Willie, who was standing near Mother, said, 'You won't need to. I'll take Ella home.' When Ella heard this she rose quickly, knocking down the orange box, and jumped right over Mother's enamel bucket of water.

'You dirty young midden!' Mother shouted at her. 'I have a good mind to throw the water about you.'

'What the hell have I done wrang noo?' Ella asked her. 'What have you done wrang?' Mother echoed. 'If you didnae ken that it's wrang to jump wi' your dirty petticoats oot ower folks' clean water, it's about time you did.'

'You daft bitch! I niver touched the water,' Ella went on.

This was too much for Mother. She lifted the bucket and

73

threw the contents over the poor girl. 'I'll put some sense into you, one way or anither, lassie,' Mother told her.

All of us were rather surprised at Mother. I had expected her to laugh and shake her head at the girl. So I scanned her face, and saw that my mother was not so well. 'Ma, you should have let me fetch the water.' My voice was anxious now.

'I'm aa right, lassie. Take that cor into the tent and put something dry on her.'

I shouted to Ella who was still squealing like a stuck pig. 'You had better put this on,' I told her, when we were inside the tent, handing her some dry clothes.

'Ee, ye bugger! I never thochd she wad dae't. I'm fair drookit. Tell Willie nae tae gang awa'. I'll no' be a meenit.'

Ella was into the dry clothes in little more than a minute, then she dashed out and across to where Willie stood. Then to the astonishment of his parents and the others he walked away with her.

'Hye, min!' his father shouted after him. 'Come back here!'

Ella turned around and waved, but Willie just ignored his father's command, and soon they were out of sight in the darkness. Uncle Geordie started to rave about what he would do to Willie when he came back. 'I'll grind him into atoms!' was the least of his threats. Annie too added her convictions. 'I will never look on him as a brother of mine again.' Aunt Martha looked speechless and bewildered. Most of the others were directing pitying glances at me. Idiots, I thought, and looked at Mother who winked slyly, her lips holding back a smile. Her wink told me not to protest, and also that now I was free, rid of his unwanted advances.

Later in bed she lay on her side smoking and told me that she was pleased with me for keeping silent. 'They would have been wildly angry with you, and would have blamed you for making their boy go off with that girl.'

'I ken, Ma, but I don't like them all thinking that he has scorned me for that silly lassie. That is what they think. All of them.'

'Aye, and he doesn't want them to know that you turned

him down. So that was his way of getting out of it. Now he is still The Man. Pride and arrogance—that's his trouble. Do you want to be ruled by pride too?'

'No, but. . . .' I began.

'Nae buts,' Mother interrupted. 'Be sensible.'

'If she has any sense she would take that laddie,' Katie put in.

'You take him then,' I told her.

'You couldn't find a better-looking laddie in a month's travel,' Katie continued, 'and aa his folk think the world of you.'

'Wheesht, lassies, any more the night.'

'Ma,' Katie said in a lower, more pleasant voice, 'I don't want you going oot to work the morn.'

'Neither do I, Ma,' I put in. 'You're no' just yourself, are you?'

'Well, I could be better, but it's nothing to worry about.'

'You're no' gaen, Ma,' Katie told her. 'We are not going to let you.'

Lexy, who was sleeping at mother's back, began to stir and make little squeaky noises. 'Go and sleep,' Mother told us, and we did.

Next morning I rose early, but Annie had already got the fire going and the kettles and cans on. 'I never babbit an eye the whole night,' she greeted me. 'I just cannae believe that a brother of mine could do such a thing.'

Then I noticed a wee tent made of sacking. 'Wha's in there?' I asked. 'It's him, the bam, that's in there. Mammy told him that he was not to sleep with his brothers after being away wi' that other bam. I wouldn't allow him to drink out of the dishes either. I gave him his tea in a jeely-jar. Daddy is going to make him scarify himself in the burn as soon as he gets up.' Travelling people often call their parents Daddy and Mammy, even when they are grown up.

'How could Willie go with that dirty tail when he had the chance of a fine lassie like you? I was so happy at the thought of having you in the family.' Tears clouded her eyes as she spoke.

'It's not his fault, Annie,' I began, feeling a bit guilty. Then, recovering, I said, 'Ella was throwing herself at him.'

'She was throwing herself at aa the laddies as well as him. That's nae excuse. I will never feel the same towards him. Shame and pride are making you hide your feelings, Betsy. I can understand that. I'll never forgive him. Never, never, never!'

I felt like a very small confused earth-worm, not sure which stone to wriggle under.

Our tea can was boiling. So I put the tea into it, then carried it over to our tent, and gave Mother a cup of tea in bed. 'Somebody's affie clever this morning,' Mother said. Usually it was Mother herself who got up and made the tea. 'You will bide at the camp today, Ma, won't you?' I asked her.

'I suppose I could,' she answered.

Mother didn't like staying off work, because the money was shared equally—every family getting the same amount, even although some families had more and some fewer workers. We were all the one breed and so we considered ourselves as one big family. The young men who scythed every day never quibbled about this.

Hearing voices raised in anger, Mother said, 'I suppose that's Willie getting the works from his father.'

'Ma, it's a shame,' I answered her. 'I should tell them the truth.'

'If you do, Betsy, he will be hurt a thousand times worse. He must have his pride. So let it be.'

I knew then that she was right.

'Aye, poor laddie, his pride will be a sair burden to him if he disnae throw the half o' it awa'.' Mother sighed as she spoke.

We finished the cornfield that day. The last sheaves were bound and stooked by mid-afternoon.

We were the only family which lived in a house in the winter. The others intended to stay on at that farm to gather the farmer's potatoes and pull his turnips. They would build sturdy bow tents and gailies to winter in. Gailies, or barricades as some called them, were high and strong constructions, attached to the tents. The fire would be set in the middle of this gailie, so a hole was left in the middle of the roof to let the smoke out through an improvised chimney made of tin. It was warm and cosy inside, and as those structures were round-shaped, lots of people could sit round the fire.

Mother had been as busy, if not more so, as she would have been in the field. When we came home from work I could see our blankets, sheets, and covers dancing on wire ropes put up between the trees. She had washed them at the burn. 'Ma!' Katie rebuked her, 'you should have taken a rest.'

'Ach, dinnae fash yoursel' lassie. There's nothing much wrang wi' me.'

'When are you gaen hame, Aunt Maggie?' Annie asked her.

'I'll wait till my brother Jimmie comes back,' Mother answered. Uncle Jimmie had set off with his pipes in his oxter two days earlier and had not as yet returned.

'Oh! Well, in that case you could be here long enough. I have seen him no' coming back for two or three weeks. He will have met some of the rest of them and be drinking with them.' Mother had fourteen brothers travelling around the highlands of Perthshire.

'We will miss you aa when we do go hame,' Mother told Annie.

'After what that stupid brother o' mine did to your lassie, you should be glad to get away from us. I never thought that it was in him to do such a thing.' Annie was still smarting.

Mother turned her head sideways and slipped me a wink before answering Annie. 'Ach, it's no' as if they were going about together. I think she will survive.'

32

Just then the sound of a child screaming in agony, and the anxious screeching of other bairns, came to our ears. Annie and I ran like hares towards the wood and found little Tommy lying writhing on the ground under a tree. 'He fell down off that branch!' the weans were shouting, some of them crying in distress.

All the others too had come running and, just as Annie was going to lift the bairn up, Mother shouted, 'Leave him!' She then went over to Tommy and felt his legs. 'Is your back sore, Tommy,' she asked, 'or your head?'

'No,' he sobbed.

'Your neck: can you move your neck, wean?'

'It's sore!' he screamed, but could move his neck.

Mother ran her hand over him. 'I think he has knocked out his shoulder-bone. Aye, it is out of the socket. Wha was supposed to be looking after the weans? My God! His mother will be in some state when she comes home.'

Hendry had taken his wife and my aunts into the village to shop. Toosh's girl Phemie who was thirteen had been left in charge of the weans. Lexy had gone with Hendry too, to fetch a few things for Mother.

'Where is Phemie?' Annie asked.

'She run away through the wood when she heard you all coming,' one of the bairns answered.

Mother had little Tommy on his feet now. He was pale and evidently in pain. Mother was supporting the painful arm. 'Your daddy will take you to a doctor as soon as he comes home,' Mother told him.

'I'm no' gaen near ony silly doctor,' Tommy cried, and started to scream again. 'He'll tak' me away fae my mammie and daddy and put me in a hospital.'

Then Hendry and Jean came running through the trees, looking very anxious.

'He's all right,' Mother shouted to them.

'I'll tak' you in the van to the doctor,' Hendry said.

'No, I said no! I'm no' gaen to any doctor.'

'You'll have to, Tommy,' his mother pleaded.

'No, Ma. Please, Ma. It's no' sore now.'

Travellers were all scared of doctors, and the bairns were terrified of them. They had heard so many tales of burkers and body-snatchers.

78

'We cannae mend your shoulder. You will have to see a doctor. Come!' his father said, lifting the boy up.

Tommy twisted and wriggled himself out of his father's arms screaming. 'No, Daddy! Please no, Daddy! No! No!'

'My God, he is going to break something else,' his father said. 'All right Tommy, we'll no' bother wi' a doctor.'

They took him to the camp and Mother wound a scarf around his upper arms, holding the bone into the socket.

'That's fine. It's better now,' the bairn grunted through his teeth. His fear of doctors greater than his intense pain, he was trembling like a leaf in a breeze.

Then Toosh asked, 'Where's Phemie?' We had all forgotten about her.

'It wasnae her fault,' Tommy got out. 'She told me not to go up that tree. I hurried up it when her back was turned.'

All the young ones set off through the woods to look for Phemie. We knew that she would be hiding somewhere, feeling really awful. Rounding some bushes I bumped into Willie, and was about to run off.

'Wait a minute, Betsy,' he said in a pleading voice.

I looked into his eyes and my heart almost melted. There was real misery there in Willie's eyes.

'Betsy, I am a fool,' he said, 'the biggest fool walking. You might have come to like me in time.'

'I do like you, Willie,' I answered, 'but not that way.'

'I am mad, mad,' he went on. 'There is nae other word for it.'

Then Lexy came running up to us. 'I think I ken whaur Phemie is hiding,' she cried. 'There's a hollow tree down this way,' Lexy went on. 'We sometimes hide in it when we play hide and seek.'

We followed her, and sure enough that's where Phemie was. Willie asked her who she was hiding from and helped her out of the tree.

She was sobbing and trembling. 'Is wee Tommy hurt?' she asked, 'Mammy will be my death. I'm sorry.'

I took her in my arms. 'Tommy's all right,' I told her.

Then, knowing that the others would be scattered through

the wood looking for her, I opened my mouth and called 'Loo-ral!' as loud as I could, several times.

Willie laughed at this and gave a whistle which I am sure could have been heard a mile away.

Soon the others all came. Toosh, having been a bit anxious about Phemie, refrained from chiding her. Little Tommy was sleeping fitfully in his granny's arms. I knew that she was cramped sitting there holding him, yet she wouldn't make the slightest move to disturb him.

Annie and I ran all the way to the farm for the milk and told Mrs McPherson why we were late. Ella, as bold as brass, said, 'Haud on a minute. I'm nearly finished and I'll come wi ye.'

'Indeed you will not,' Annie told her. Then turning to Mrs McPherson, said, 'You will have to keep that lassie away from the camp. Otherwise we will all have to leave.'

'What has the limmer been up to?' the farmer's wife asked. Here Ella butted in, saying, 'Well, if I'm no' getting tae come tae the camp, tell Willie I'll meet him at the big tree.'

'That's what she's up to, Mrs McPherson, and my daddy says that we cannae be responsible for what might happen to her. So if she does come back to the camp, we will just bundle and go.'

'Dinnae fear. I'll see that she'll no bother you again,' the farmer's wife told us.

Then she knitted her brows and said, 'Oh aye, I mind what I was going to tell you. There's a bone-setter about a mile and a half from here. Do you see yon shepherd's house awa' ower yonder? Abeen yon field o tatties. It's no' far across the fields, but you will likely have tae gang roon the road. He is very clever wi' bones and a grand piper as weel. He is called Rory McDonald. His wife is a fine body tae. Tak' the young lad up tae him.'

'Oh thank you. We will. If you'll excuse us we'll hurry hame to let them ken.'

When we returned to the camp Uncle Jimmie, looking a bit under the weather, was sitting with Tommy on his knee. Annie quickly told them about the bone-setter and where he lived.

'We will take Tommy there now,' Jean said.

'I'm coming wi' my bairn.' Uncle Jimmie adored wee Tommy, and always called him his bairn. Hendry started the van and away they went.

33

Mother was getting ready to go back to Brechin, throwing away anything that she wasn't taking home with her. It would all be burnt the next day. 'We are gaen hame the morn. Hendry is taking us in his van,' she told me. I had very mixed feelings about going home. I would miss them all.

Later we all gathered round the open fire and talked in the way that we were wont to before a parting. There was a certain melancholy in our words and voices. Would we all ever be together again? Our hearts were big and open to each other. Ricky came and sat leaning against my legs, as if he knew that the wonderful freedom which he had enjoyed here was almost over.

Tommy's bantam cock began to crow in the peculiar way that bantams do. 'Wheesht, you silly bird. We're no' wantin' rain the morn.' Mother's words broke the spell of melancholy. 'Did any o' ye ever pay attention to what that bird says?' she continued. When we shook our heads or made a guess she said, 'Well, I'll tell you. Every morning when I am putting on my claes it shouts "I-can-see-you". Listen to it now if you don't believe me. "I-can-see-you." Hear it?' Then we were all laughing.

'Jean and Hendry seem to be taking an awful long time,' an anxious Martha said.

'Why did Uncle Jimmy come back?' I asked her.

'He says that something told him to come back, and I can well believe him. He just dotes on that wee laddie.'

'Here they come,' Uncle Geordie said, and soon Jean was battered with questions.

'You will be wondering what kept us,' Jean answered. 'We

had to wait till McDonald finished a pibroch. When we got to the house and heard the pipes Uncle Jimmie nearly went mad. "Now that's what I call piping," he said. "Oh, bairn, I wish you were not so sore. We daren't disturb him. He must be practising for the games." The silly man wouldn't let us disturb the piper,' Jean went on. 'I think he really wanted to hear the playing.

'Then after we had sat at the gate for a while the woman happened to see us through the window, and she came out. Well, tak' what we got from Rory McDonald. "Would you keep that wean out there in agony? Do you think that I am some kind of brutal devil? Do you think that I would put my piping before a dear wee lamb suffering pain?" Oh, he gave us the works. Then without a word of warning, he gave the bairn's arm a quick jerk which made him howl blue murder. Then he petted the wean, and gave him a two shilling bit. "That's it all over, Tommy. Your arm is back in its place now. Soon you will be as right as rain," he told him.

'I asked what he wanted for his kind services, and he nearly ate me. "Na, Na," he said. "I paid nothing for the gift and I'm no' gae'n tae charge for doing it. It was free tae me, and I'll give it free to them that need it."'

34

Next morning I got up at the peep o' day. I wanted to get my hair washed and bathe in the burn. My dress too needed washing. I had intended doing it all the night before, but with all the excitement about Tommy, I hadn't bothered. Lifting Mother's empty water bucket, I walked lightly past the tents of the others.

The little spring bubbling up at the bottom of the burn was quite a bit away from the camp. Annie and I had dammed all around it, and deepened the bottom, so that we could lift the water more easily. The sun was still wading through a grey mist, so I decided to take the water back to the camp before washing my hair. The burn water was ice cold and I didn't fancy dipping my head into it until the sun had won her way through.

I sat down on a stone. The very early morning was, and still is, my favourite time of day. Especially in the country. The music of the burn, of the birds, and the occasional little squeaky noises of mice or voles in the grass, were so pleasant and soothing to my ears. Then I lifted my eyes and sniffed the air whilst I gazed around me. Wild mint gave the air a tang, a delicious tang which seemed to enter my bloodstream as I breathed it in. The serene beauty was filling my eyes and every sense I possessed was gorging itself. My very soul lifted.

I was so engrossed with nature that footsteps on the stones behind me made me jump.

'It's only me!'

I recognised Annie's voice.

'What are you doing sitting there all alone?' she continued.

'Oh I was just thinking deep thoughts,' I told her, knowing that Annie would never understand my love affair with nature.

Then I rose up, and there was Ricky bounding towards me. I spoke to him in a low voice and laid my hand on his head. 'I let him out,' Annie told me. 'I couldnae sleep for thinking about you going away today. I saw you leaving the camp. I was sitting in the front of Hendry's van. Betsy, you could stay here with us. Ask your mother.'

'No, Annie,' I replied. 'Mother's not looking very well. I couldn't leave her.'

'Jean told me what's wrong with her,' Annie said. 'Women of your mum's age go through something which they call the change of life. It goes on for a long time and when it is finished they don't have periods any more, but it's not serious.'

'Every woman?' I asked her.

'Aye,' she answered, 'just like every girl takes them at a certain age, they go away again at a certain age.'

Traveller women at that time kept their children very much in the dark about those things. The poor boys were even worse than the girls. No woman or girl dare talk about any of the peculiarities of a woman's body, child-bearing included, in front of men or children. With older travelling people, this still is upheld. No talk of 'women's way of doing', as they call it, dare be uttered within the earshot of men. These customs were very strictly adhered to, so that many young men and girls were very ignorant indeed.

Annie's explanation of mother's slight under-the-weather look was quite news to me. 'Jean says that it affects your whole body.' Annie showed that she was proud of her wordly knowledge, as she spoke.

Back at the camp we prepared tea and went round all the tents giving all the adults a cupful in bed. By then the sun had warmed the earth. So I washed my hair, and my dress, and helped Lexy to get her hair done. It was very long and thick. Out here in the country one could go about a bit wild like nature, but where nature was tamed and covered with cement, tar and stones, one had to look tamed too. In the town the earth was considered to be coarse, common, and filthy. It was indelicate to see a spot of it on anyone's clothes or shoes. Silly folk, I thought, didn't they know that everything needed for their material well-being came from the earth, and everything beneficial to their spiritual well-being too? Not that I would like to see a house or a street full of earth, but I can't see it as filth.

Wee Tommy was much easier after a good sleep, and he asked his dad if he could come with us to Brechin in the van. So after goodbyes which left us all a bit dowie we were on our way.

35

Hendry only stayed long enough in the house to have a bite to eat and a cup of tea. We were all rather quiet that evening and, after the beds were made and the other chores seen to, I felt so lonely and restless. Ricky lay under the table, his brown eyes following my every move.

'Ma! I'm going to take the dog out for a walk. If the neighbours tell the Council, that is just too bad. I cannae bear to see him like that.'

'You'd better put on his lead, and dinnae be lang.' Mother knew that time slipped sleekitly away from me.

Ricky's joy at getting out of the house was better expressed than mine. He was all the company that I wanted. So I was pleased when Lexy said that she was staying to play with a girl who lived next door.

As I opened the gate a young sailor and a girl that I knew came walking down the pavement. 'Andy!' I exclaimed. 'Is it really you?' and 'Hello Sheelah,' to the girl. He was a big lad and would have picked me up and tossed me in the air but for Ricky's warning growl.

'Oh! so I daurnae meddle,' Andy laughed. 'You're gaen tae be an auld maid, Betsy, if you don't put awa' that pot-licker.'

'If you are as brave a sailor as you are with wee pet dogs, then God help the Navy, Andy Middleton,' I ragged him back. The three of us tossed jocular words at one another for a few minutes.

'I have just taken Sheelah for to taste my stovies,' Andy said.

'Stovies?' I echoed, 'Is that the latest word for it?'

'If it wasnae for fear of your mongrel tearing these claes, I would gie you your tatties withoot being stoved. This claes are no' mine, ye ken. They belong tae the King. Oh, and speaking aboot the King, I hear he has gotten a bit o' stuff to himself at last. Some yankee woman.'

Andy's talk about the King was news to me. I hadn't read a newspaper for months. 'That's great,' I exclaimed.

'His mother and all the rest o' the family doesnae think that it's great,' Sheelah told me. 'She's a married woman, or maybe she is divorced. Anyway there is an affie screech aboot it in aa the papers.'

When they walked away Andy stepped out proudly in his uniform. He had broadened out, and really looked so different from the poor laddie whose mother had reared a large family on her own, and had worked hard in the fields to do so. Andy had become adept at making stovies when he came home from school, and was for ever proudly telling us about his super stovies. If he didn't turn up when we used to play games, we would say, 'Oh Andy will be makin' stovies.' Hence the joke about the stovies.

Before I knew it I was standing on the old bridge across the South Esk river. My feet had taken the lead, whilst my mind was absent. It had wandered back to the encampment. Once again I experienced the long stare with which Willie had held my eyes. It had not been the stare of soft love, but an accusing look of frustration. So I dismissed that thought. Then Annie's heartfelt tears as she plied me with her prettiest clothes. Jean's light-hearted joking farewells, I knew, had been a cover for her vexation at parting with us. The look in the eyes of my aunts, uncles, other cousins, and half-cousins belied their cheery words of parting. Lexy's appeal for a kiss from Tommy had been scornfully refused amidst laughter from the others.

Yes, I was going to miss them all terribly, I thought, as I tried to retrieve my mind and my heart, which had also sped out to them. Then I wandered along the road just after crossing the bridge, until I came to a little spring-well at the side of the road. I knew almost every tree and bush that skirted this road, having walked it so often with my father. He used to cut willow wands to make baskets with, telling me strange tales and stories as we sat stripping the bark off the willows. Once, when my ill-fitting shoes had skinned my heels, he had bathed my feet at this spring well, and tore a piece off his shirt tail to bind them with.

How can I sit here and recall these things without shedding tears? I thought. Instead of this warm, pleasant feeling, I should be going mad with grief.

Before I had time to think of an answer, the sound of horses' hooves made me turn my head in their direction.

Travellers, I thought. They must be staying out at Pow Soddies. This was the name of a camp a mile or two out on the road.

The man, recognising me, reined in the pony. 'You're Maggie's lassie, are ye no'? Is there anybody with you?'

'No,' I answered him, 'only Ricky my dog.'

'You shoudnae be wandering your lee-leaf-alane like that. Anybody could attack you,' he told me.

'Ach, you are as bad as my mother,' I said. 'Ricky would tear anyone to pieces who looked the wrong way at me.'

His wife and five children were in the cart with him, and a young lad of about thirteen, the oldest, was cycling behind the cart. Their few belongings were under a tent-cover.

'Are you shifting?' I asked.

'We had tae shift,' the woman told me. 'Sympathy was there yesterday and when he came back today and seen that we were still there, he wasnae very pleased.' 'Sympathy' of course was the local policeman I mentioned earlier.

'I'm affie sorry, and ye hae my sympathy, but you'll hae tae gang.' She mocked the policeman. 'As sure as death, lassie,' she continued, 'he made us pull doon the tent and throw everything into the yoke. And me just gaen awa' tae mak' a bite o' supper tae the weans. And me after trailing aboot on my feet aa day looking for a bite to them. God pity Sympathy, but I suppose the cratur has tae dae what he is telt.'

'Whar are ye bound for noo?' I asked.

'It'll just have tae be Lightnin' Hill. Jump in and we'll give you a hurl hame.'

I shouted to Ricky who did not hesitate to jump up beside us. I am not going to mention the name of that family, because all of the children are now house-dwellers, and living just like non-travellers, trying to hide the fact that they came of travelling people. They would be furious if I gave them away.

There are a great deal of travellers like-minded. Some go as far as to shun their own brothers or sisters who still retain some of the traveller ways, traditions and language. This is the cause of much sorrow amongst older travelling people. The fact that there is no need to behave like that nowadays does not deter them.

87

At that time there was no free way to a high standard of education, except if one was really brilliant. Nurses, teachers and other such workers, had to pay for their training and were very highly regarded. So there was a great majority who just took the word of others like themselves. Just went by what they were told, in other words. They didn't bother looking to see, or trying to find out, whether what they were told was right or the the truth.

So we travelling people were judged without knowledge. Every crime, sin, foulness, acts of violence, cruelty, stupidity, and brutish behaviour under the sun was, to their way of thinking, the heritage of all travelling people. Some of this still lingers yet in the minds of a minority of people—those without the ability to think for themselves, or to believe what they can see with their own eyes.

Certainly all travellers had much the same traditions, but every family had their own peculiarities, which all other travellers knew about. So that if the peculiarities of, say, the Camerons were displeasing to the Reids, they could avoid each other. The reason why these peculiarities were kept within families was because of their habit of marrying within their own breed.

However, I have wandered. I had better return to where the sturdy little garron pony was pulled up, near our house, to allow me to get off. I waved goodbye to the driver and family from the gate of our house.

That will keep me busy tomorrow, I thought, as I looked at the masses of weeds in the garden, and the almost waist-high grass on the drying green.

'Ma, did you keep Daddy's scythe?' I asked Mother as soon as I entered the house.

'Not me,' she answered. 'What would we want with a scythe.'

'To cut that grass,' I told her. 'There's a huke in the shed. That will do as well.'

She was making girdle scones and made a mock swipe at me as I darted off with one.

36

So the following day Lexy and I got busy in the garden. We made a fun thing of it, laughing and larking about. We looked up when a voice from over the dyke said, 'You're busy,' and we saw Bryce Whyte, the young man I mentioned earlier.

'Well, dinnae stand there like a coo lookin' ower a dyke. Come in and lend a hand.' My heart went out to him as he hastened with evident pleasure to do my teasingly given bidding. I shoved a push-hoe into his hands, but within five minutes I realised that all green growth was weeds to Bryce. 'Maybe I should get you to cut the grass,' I told him.

Then I asked where he was staying.

'We are staying up at a farm near Kirriemuir.'

'Kirriemuir?' I echoed. 'What are you doing down here?'

'My sister is up at Lightning Hill, and I have been coming down to stay with her every weekend.' Lightning Hill was a camping site near Brechin.

'You dinnae believe in short cuts, do you?' I went on.

He blushed and said, 'Well, I have been coming this way every week, looking to see if you were home.'

'So you have just come from Kirriemuir then?' When he nodded, I asked him to come into the house for a cup of tea.

'Is your mother in?' he asked.

'Aye,' I answered, 'but she has already had something to eat. So you are safe enough.'

Mother rarely needed to ask questions. So she came out of the kitchen almost immediately with a bowl of tea and some sandwiches. Handing them to Bryce she said, 'I saw you through the window.'

'He is going to cut the grass,' I told her.

'Oh! So that's what he came here for?' Mother's eyes were twinkling as she spoke.

Bryce laughed and blushed. 'I wanted to ask you if I could take Betsy to the pictures tonight.' It was very obvious that he had had to make a great effort to get this out.

'Well, now. I'm no sae sure aboot that,' Mother rather gravely answered. After a pause during which the changing expressions on Bryce's face were comical to behold she said, 'You had better ask Betsy.' Then, taking pity on the poor lad, she went out to the shed to get the huke.

'I've lookit for you lang and sair every weekend,' Bryce told me. 'I just cannae stop thinkin' aboot ye. Will ye come wi' me? I'll tak' ye richt hame.'

I told Bryce that if he made a good job of cutting the grass, I would consider going with him to the pictures.

'Never mind the grass,' he said. 'Say that you'll come.'

His eyes lit up when I nodded.

Mother was sharpening the huke at the door. 'I'll do that,' he told her. Lexy, who was still skilfully hoeing and weeding, straightened her back and looking towards me held out the hoe.

'Aye, I'm coming,' I called.

If Bryce had difficulty telling weeds from flowers, he had none with the grass, and soon had it level enough to get it mowed. 'The day is runnin' awa',' I told him. 'Your sister will be wondering what's keeping you.'

'Aye, I will away noo, but I'll be back about seven o'clock.'

It was Laurel and Hardy in a film called *Bonny Scotland* which was on that night and there were parts of it that I could scarcely see, with the power of laughter-tears which blinded me. Bryce did bring me home then stayed for a cup of tea before going to his sister.

'Can I come in to see you on my way home tomorrow?' he asked, when I went to the door with him. 'I usually go walking with Lexy on Sundays,' I answered. 'We just can't sit about the house all day. If you want to you can look in next weekend.' I gave his bike a push as I spoke.

How-an-ever, Bryce was to find the house empty again the following weekend. A farmer we had worked for before came to the door and asked if we could possibly come and help with his potato harvest. Mother was a bit reluctant. 'I have lost Sandy since I last saw you,' she told the farmer, 'and it is not easy living out in the cold weather without a man to get sticks, and build accommodation.'

After expressing his sympathy for our loss, the farmer pressed Mother to come. 'I will give you an empty cottar house,' he said, 'and plenty coals and paraffin. I'm really stuck for workers this year.'

On this, Mother agreed.

The farmer's name was Patullo and he owned more than one farm in the Kirriemuir district. The name of the farm was Linross and the road going up to it was and still is just opposite Glamis Castle.

37

So the next day Mother put her foot on the train and went to see our Aunt Jean in Blairgowrie. Aunt Jean was also a widow with four of a family. She had been married to one of Mother's brothers, and she herself was my father's sister.

Travelling people liked to marry into their own breed. A breed was usually two or perhaps three names. Our breed was made up of Johnstones, Townsleys, and Reids. They had inter-married for generations, knew their faults and weaknesses, also their good points, and did not like any person marrying into another breed. Some did, of course, but could be made to feel rather uncomfortable. In-laws on both sides could be rather critical. Every breed was very distinctive and recog-nisable, even to non-travellers who were familiar with them. This is no longer the case.

Anyway, Mother had gone to Blairgowrie to ask Jean and her family to come to Linross with us. Mother and Jean were great pals so she readily agreed, and came back to Brechin in the train with Mother. Their few worldly possessions— blankets, dishes and clothes—had been packed into an old pram, and were put in the guard's van. Nothing was charged for it. Lexy and I eagerly went to meet the train. We knew that it would be the first one after dark.

Jean's daughter was just months younger than me, and we adored each other's company. Katie and Jean's oldest daughter, also called Katie, were also about ages, and great pals. Her other two were boys, Jimmie the oldest and Willie who was about Lexy's age. After warm greetings, they spent the night with us. Few of us slept much, we had so much to talk about.

A friend who had an old car with a trailer agreed to take us up, for a small fee. Can you believe that he only made one journey? Eight somehow got crammed inside the car with our belongings, and Jessie and I inside the trailer. We lay on our backs on top of blankets and a tarpaulin was tied down on top of us. We covered our heads with it when going through Forfar. Of course we waited for the cover of darkness before leaving Brechin.

We knew where the old cottar was, so in a few minutes we had our bits and pieces into it. Then Jessie and I went to a straw soo which stood at the edge of a field, to fetch straw for our bedding. A soo was a huge house-shaped stack, and could be of hay or straw. The hay ones were thatched with straw, or covered with tarpaulins. At that time a lot of straw and hay were used on farms. Meanwhile the two Katies and Jimmie went for water and coals.

'Be sure to knock on the bothy door, and tell the ploughmen that you have permission from the farmer to take the coals,' Mother warned Jimmie. 'They ploughmen lads will soon mak' short work o' ye if you don't. They might think you are stealing it.'

Then Aunt Jean spoke to the two Katies. 'You twa lassies, hide yourselves round the side o' the bothy, and if they pluchies get ower rough wi' Jimmie, then the two of you go up to them. Otherwise keep yourselves hidden.'

The Forfarshire ploughmen at that time were notorious for their ill-tricks, and travelling people were fair game to practise them on. They were a good bunch of lads really. Their lot was hard toil and deprivation so to relieve the monotony of their lives they seized on any diversion that came along, in the only way known to them.

The house was a but-and-ben with a little room in the middle. One big room had a stone floor, and the other two floors were wooden. Mother told Aunt Jean to take the room with the wooden floor as it would be warmer. Jessie and I teased the straw and made the beds, whilst Mother and Jean got everything in place, and rummaged some sticks to make a fire. This was all done by candle-light. Then we waited long and long for the girls and Jimmie to come back. 'Na, na, we are not going to get a sup of tea tonight,' Aunt Jean said. 'We will have to go up and see what's keeping them.'

Just then we heard the souch of them coming and the noise of the coals being dropped at the door. Jimmie's first words were, 'If you want any more coals, you will have to go and fetch them yourselves. I am not going back about they moich pluchies.' His face was very red from exertion.

The two lassies put down the buckets of water and amidst giggles told us why they had taken so long. 'Mammy dear, you would have died laughing.'

Both the Katies were talking together, so Mother said, 'Wheesht, and let Jimmie tell us.'

'Well,' Jimmie began, 'I was just gaen towards the bothy door when this pluchie came ower from the steading wi' a lantern in his hand. God forgie me for remarking on it, and God bless the dear man, but he has twa lugs that would mak a pair o' blankets. "The farmer said that we could get some coals," I told him. "Oh aye," says he, "you'll be ane o' they lads that's come tae dae the tatties." I answered him "Aye." Then says he, "I'll tell ye what. If you can put my back tae the ground, I'll gie ye as much coal as ye can carry."

'Now by this time the bothy door had opened and another six big pluchies were standing round the door. They had heard us speaking. "That's a fair enough offer," one o' them said.

' "I suppose it is," says I, "but there's seven o' ye and I'm just mysel."

' "Oh but we're no lads like that. We'll gie ye fair play. It's only Luggie that ye'll hae tae wassle wi'."

'I could see Luggie mair clearly now, in the light of the open door, and I thought tae mysel', I'm doing weel, having noticed that he was thick-witted. As ye ken, they thick-witted folk sometimes have the strength of the Auld Ruchie. "Could ye no' just gie me the bit coal, and I'll come up some other time to wassle wi' ye?" I was desperately trying to get out o' it. Ah! but they weren't gaen tae tak' no for an answer. "Well, well, then," says I, "Let's get on wi' it. Dinnae blame me if ye land in the hospital." At the same time I was quaking wi' the dead fright.

'However, as God would have it, I soon found out that he was one o' they big soft craturs that couldnae knock the flour off a bap. Was I no' glad. The others were aa round about us shouting, "Come on, Luggie, dae yer stuff, man." One o' them was holding up the lantern. I let him pull and haul me aboot for a while, then, here goes, I says tae mysel'.

'I got his head in my oxter and my knee on his spine and I downed him. Then I sprung on top of him and pinned him to the ground. "Ye bugger, ye've broken my eggs!" he shouted.

' "Eggs?" says I.

' "Aye, my bloody eggs, ye damn tink bugger."

'Then I noticed that my knees were sodden wi' the yolks of eggs. His jacket pockets must have been full of eggs. He must have been coming back after pinching them when I met him. "I'm real sorry aboot your eggs, Luggie," I told him, rising and helping him up. "You're a gey tough lad."

'He was very deflated now and I really felt sorry for him. I am sure that the tears were in his eyes as he went on about the eggs. "It's nae often that I get the chance o' a pickle eggs. That sciffy has een like a hawk when she's gathering them, but she missed that nest. I spotted them the day."

' "Look, Luggie," I said, taking a half-crown out of my pocket, "tak' this and buy yourself some eggs at the farm."

' "Na, na," he said, "I cannae tak' your money."

' "I have tons o' money," I told him. "I've been working at the hairst." In the end I got him to tak' the half-crown. So that was that.

'However, when I went to where the coal was lying in an open cart shed just next tae the bothy, one o' the other

94

pluchies shouted to me. "Just haud on a meenite. You're no' gettin' awa' as easy as that. I'll fill a bag for ye, and if ye can lift it on yer back and carry it awa', then it's yours."

' "That's fair enough," another one shouted.

'Then they went and got a big grain sack, and between the lot o' them filled it wi' coal in a few minutes. "Now, let's see ye put that on your back and carry it off."

'I'll guarantee you, that there was mair than twa hundred-weight in the bag.

' "I honestly couldnae move that sack," I told him, "but I'll tell ye what I'll dae wi' you." You see I kent they liked a challenge. "You are aa big strappin' men," I went on. "So, the amount that the strongest o' ye can lift and carry, I will take that. And if I cannae, then I will want coal. Now I think that that is fair enough."

' "Well spoken, lad. Come on, Geordie, you try first."

'So I had to wait until they aa had a go. It's a good thing that I am used to lifting heavy scrap and bags o' grain. I just managed by the skin o' my teeth to lift and carry the bag that the strongest one carried. I'm fair forfochen wi' it. There must be twelve stone in it.' Jimmie looked forfochen too.

'We held up the bottom o' the bag, coming down the road,' the Katies put in.

'Aye,' Jimmie said, 'and a good job too.'

'Did the pluchies see you two?' Mother asked the girls.

'No, they went into the bothy. We helped him down the road then went back for the water.'

We ate later and went to bed early as we were going to work the next day. I found sleep difficult because of the heart-searing, doleful lowing of calves which had been newly separated from their mothers. Why did I have to feel so intensely about that sort of thing, I wondered. Why did it disturb me so profoundly, causing restlessness and melancholy? To this day I still haven't found the answer to that question.

Anyway, that night I groped for Mother's pipe, lit it, and soothed myself with the power of tobacco.

38

Next morning, Mother and Jean got up when the cocks crew. We used no clocks. The work was no trouble at all to us. We had been on tattie fields almost since birth, our mothers working with us secured snugly under a thick plaid on their backs.

I loved the smell of newly turned earth, and the field was amass with poppies, scentless violets, and wild mint. The mint showed its displeasure at being crushed and uprooted by exuding its pleasing fragrance very strongly.

Jean and Mother, the two Katies, Jessie and me, and Willie and Lexy sort of paired, and laughter was heard from us almost all day. Jessie and I romped and rolled on the earth, as did Willie and Lexy. We didn't worry about being all earthy as long as it was dry.

Jimmie was content to joke with the ploughmen. He worked on the carts which took the potatoes off the fields to the pits. There were no jarring mechanical noises. Just the snorting of horses—mostly Clydesdales or Shires—and the sound of their hooves or the occasional commands to the animals from the ploughmen.

Jimmie sometimes took his pipes up to the bothy at nights. One lad had a concertina, another a mouth organ, and when they tired of playing they would sit and tell jokes or crack about different things.

We worked a half day only on Saturdays. Then all of us walked into Kirriemuir. As we passed Glamis Castle, Mother said, 'God forbid that I would have to live in that place.'

'They say that it is haunted, Ma. Do you think that's true?' I asked her.

'Well I dinnae ken about that, but I do ken that there are plenty haunted stories about it. Do you see yon highest parapet? Well, they say that lang, lang ago the young daughter o' the place was an affy bonny lassie. Now two young knights fell in love wi' her. One was a Belmont and I'm no sure what the other one was called. Anyway, the lassie being very young carried on wi' the two o' them. She teased and kept them dangling on a string, saying that she couldnae mak' up her mind which o' them she liked the best. "I like the two o' ye just the same," she would say, and for lang and lang she kept them hanging on like this, till the two young men began to hate each other. So they decided to fight to the death for her, and Belmont, he killed the other knight in a fair fight.

'Then he went to the castle and told the lassie. She was all prettied up for the twa o' them coming and had a white rose in her hair. "Come down tae the wood and see," he said, and when she did go and did see the laddie lying there stone dead, she nearly died as well. Suddenly she realised that she loved the poor corpse covered wi' blood. "You will suffer for this," she told Belmont with the tears blinding her.

'"I never thought that you were so fond of him, or I wouldn't have killed him. Now you will never, never, be my wife," he said.

'"Never, never, let me see your face again," she replied, "or I will have you hung."

'"Will you gie me one favour?" he asked her. "That rose that's in your hair. Will you give it to me, and one wee tress of your hair? I feel bad myself now about what I've done, but I'll never, ever, tak' a wife. I love you too much." So she let him cut a tress o' her hair with his sword, and she gave him the rose. They say that a white rose, bound up wi' tresses o' hair, is the coat of arms o' the Belmonts to this day.

'Anyway this young lassie, when she wandered aboot the castle was always seeing the wraith o' the laddie that was killed. She wouldn't eat, and the doctor nor naebody else could do anything with her. "I always see him, Ma, waving for me to come to him," she kept saying. Then one morning they found her body lying all battered and bruised on the ground beneath that parapet that I showed you. They think that she seen his wraith waving to her, and that she jumped off the parapet.'

We had all been listening intently to Mother's story as we walked along. 'Dinnae crowd me so much. Surely you can hear me,' she rebuked us. We were so taken with her tale that we never felt the road, and were into Kirriemuir in what seemed a very short time.

39

Our pay did not last us long. Mother bought us all woollen gloves to pick the potatoes with and shoes for Lexy, who would soon be going back to school.

Mother denied us nothing that we desired to eat. In the evening we all went to the pictures except Mother, Aunt Jean and Jimmie. They went to a pub instead, and then met us coming out of the cinema. All of us then went to a fish and chip restaurant before getting a bus to the end of the farm road. So we would be starting work the Monday morning as rich as we had been the Monday before. In our family money was for spending as soon as it came in. We just couldn't keep it. Apart from a few families, travelling people were all like that.

We were there for a month, and really enjoyed every minute of it. There was no man in the farmhouse. The young farmer was married and lived on another farm. His mother and unmarried sister ran Linross. The old lady was a darling, young at heart and full of impish fun. Her daughter was middle-aged and was forever rebuking us for failing to take life more seriously. Our laughter and unconcern about the future, and world affairs, really rankled her. She tolerated us, rather than enjoyed our stay.

She did, however, enjoy the lecture which she never failed to give Jessie and me every evening when we went for milk. During those lectures, both of us just stood very docile and attentive out of respect, not for what she was saying but because of her position. We nodded, shook our heads or made the appropriate exclamation. Sometimes the theme would be the cruelty of bringing children into the world without proper security for them. Other times on the dangers of teasing young men.

The two Katies, Jessie and I were prone to joke amidst laughter with the young ploughmen on the fields. Even Aunt Jean and Mother joined us in this. I am sure that the lady farmer believed that we carried on with the ploughmen in the evenings. She completely misunderstood us, and thought that we were much in need of guidance. My spirit was ill-fitted to tolerate this but my sense of humour, as it often did, came to my rescue.

However, all of her speeches were not on those lines. The depression, Hitler, and the Royal Family often were her subjects, also politics. One evening she really got me interested. 'The Royal Family must be very upset with the way that the young King is carrying on,' she told us. 'It is scandalous. He should be setting an example, instead of worrying his bereaved mother, and the rest of the family. The whole world is looking on and, with respect to their distinction, they are human beings, and must be feeling very distressed about the whole thing.'

'What is he doing?' I asked her.

'What is he doing!' she almost shouted, shaking her head and forcing out a long breath of contempt for our ignorance. 'Do you mean to say that you haven't heard of his goings on with some divorced American woman? What he sees in her I'll never know. She's neither fair of face nor well-proportioned. Yet now he declares that he'll give up the throne, if they don't allow him to make her his queen.'

The old lady, her mother, put in a word here. She was standing in the doorway beside her daughter. 'If he had gotten the girl that he loved, there would have been none of this,' she said.

'Who was he in love with?' Both Jessie and I used almost the same words, at the same time, to ask the question.

'My dears, he was madly in love with Elizabeth Bowes-Lyon. You know—the young lady of Glamis Castle.'

'Mother!' her daughter interrupted. 'You are only repeating what you heard from a woman who worked at the castle.'

'I have heard it from other sources too.' The old lady was obviously annoyed at her daughter. 'If it comes to that,' she went on, "I would put more reliance on the word of a servant than on the newspapers that you read, or even your wireless.

'When Edward saw that it was useless, because of her love for his brother Albert, he said to her, "Elizabeth, I will still make you the Queen of the British Empire."' Then, turning towards her daughter, she went on, 'Can't you see that this is exactly what he intends doing? Full well he knows that the powers that be will never allow Mrs Simpson to be queen.'

'Oh Mother, you are an old blether,' her daughter told her.

The old lady, however, was determined to have the last word. 'All right then, just you wait and see.'

Jessie and I picked up the milk cans and escaped. Our mothers were always on at us for being so long away for the milk. They even teasingly accused us of having secret meetings with the young ploughmen. Mother looked me straight in the face when she said this. She had deep-seeing eyes, had Mother. Then she laughed and handed me my supper.

The lady farmer and her mother's conversation had really aroused the curiosity of Jessie and me. We talked of little else as we worked the following day. We also discussed it with Mother and Aunt Jean. 'It'll mak' little difference tae us, lassie, nae matter wha's king or wha's queen. We will still be they dirty tinkers. So dinnae worry your head about them.' Aunt Jean on saying this, changed the subject.

Mother, however, was a little more helpful. 'Well,' she said, Elizabeth is a real bonnie lassie, and it is quite possible that he is eating out his heart about her, although she is married to his brother. How-an-ever as your Aunt Jean says, what difference will it make to us?'

I determined to get a newspaper the next day that we went to the town. Believe it or not, the farmer was the only one on the farm toun, as it was called, who got a regular newspaper.

We all stayed up late the night before parting. I knew that I would miss Jessie. I could enjoy doing the tasks that I most hated, in the company of Jessie, and her presence doubled the pleasure of doing things that I liked. In every circumstance of life, I could be happy with Jessie around. I think that she felt this way too about me.

So we were reluctant to sleep away the last hours of our time together. We washed our hair and, having heated water, we scrubbed each other's backs in a zinc bath in the little middle room. However, at the actual time of parting the following day, there was much laughter and joking to cover our feelings.

Ricky was the only one who openly showed what he felt. He had so enjoyed the feeling of complete freedom to roam at will through the fields, moor and roads. He was not given to chasing cows, sheep, nor any other farm animal, so he could be allowed his freedom in the country. Eyeing our bits of things all bundled up, he guessed that it was back to the council house and to many restrictions for him. He lay on his belly looking up and turning his head from side to side as if he understood every word that was spoken. The defeated look of sadness in his eyes made me sure that he did. Or perhaps I was reading my own reflection. The reflection of my heart, in the soft brown eyes.

The house seemed cold and somehow neglected when we returned to Brechin but, after a few days when it felt the warmth of our presence, it responded beautifully and became a pleasant home again.

40

Soon the little money that Mother had when we came home ran out and, as nearly all the potatoes had been harvested, we decided to have a walk out to see a farmer who usually gave us turnip-pulling to do.

We had to pass a camping site on our way to the farm, so we went in-aboot to talk to them. A man named McQueen was busy erecting his winter tent. Another named McDonald was just putting the finishing touches to a bow-topped wagon which he had just made. Whilst Mother and Katie talked to his wife, who was big with child, Lexy and I watched the man as he deftly painted scroll-work on his wagon. This was very decorative when done.

Many traveller men had the gift for this type of painting, and were always in demand by other travellers to paint their carts and even the lorries of those fortunate enough to have lorries.

'There, that should please her now,' he said as he stepped back and gazed admiringly at his own work. We knew that he had built the wagon for his wife to have the winter baby in. She would pretty-up the inside of it by sewing curtains and making frilled pillow-cases to match. Her material would be found in some of the bags of rags which they collected.

'Come, lassies, and get a mouthful o' tea,' she called to Lexy and me. 'Sorry I don't have anything tasty to give you.' We took the proffered tea and thanked her.

There is no greater insult you can give a traveller woman, than to refuse her tea. Food you can decline to take, but she will be very hurt if tea is refused. She will take it to mean that her dishes are not clean enough for you to drink from. So tea is never refused.

She also called on the man McQueen, whose wife was away into town. 'Here's tea for you, Jimmie, you must be ready for a drop now. You've been at that tent since morning.'

'Bless you, Lena,' he said, 'my mouth is walsh for a cup o' tea.' Then the two men went to admire the wagon, taking their tea with them.

'Aye, Maggie, it's a true saying that God never made the back but what he made the burden, but yours will be a blessing to you.' I knew that the woman was referring to the recent loss of our father.

'Lassies are right and right enough,' Mother answered, 'but I could have done if one o' my laddies had been spared. Still, I could be a lot worse.' They talked for a while then we made our way to the farm. The farmer wanted his sugar-beet pulled and tapped as it had to be into the factory before Christmas, and asked us to try to get two or three more people to help. 'I'll slacken them wi' the ploo for ye,' he told Mother. Sugar-beet grows downward like carrots, and is very hard to pull out.

So I asked some of the young lads who had gone to school with me: Neil Riley, whose older brother had joined the Argyll and Sutherlands, and who could hardly wait to be old enough to join up too; Willie Kerr, who was also anxious to enlist when he reached eighteen. Robbie Thompson was the other boy who agreed to come to the beet-pulling, provided that we who had done it before would keep him right.

The farmer knew Mother very well and had given her wages in advance. Instead of being sensible with the money, we all went to the pictures with it or, rather, some of it.

Bryce was in the picture hall that night with his nephew and two brothers. Other travellers from various camping grounds around Brechin were also there, mostly men. At that time only the men were supposed to enjoy life.

Bryce immediately came over when he saw me and asked if he could sit beside me. When I nodded, he asked where we had been and when I told him he tutted and said, 'I was only about six miles away from you. I wish I had known. Can I come to see you again?'

'Do you no' want to see the picture?' I whispered.

In his excitement he was talking too loud. Then he too whispered, 'I am looking at a better picture. Can I come to your house?'

'Wheesht!' I answered.

Of course, he did become a visitor to our house, a very regular visitor. Often he was accompanied by his nephew Donald who was about my age. We more often than not all went to the pictures. Because we were an all-female family we could please ourselves about this. Mother really became addicted to the films, and enjoyed the world of make-believe.

Bryce was easy to be with, and there was no need for me to be other than myself in his presence. We all found his guile-free simplicity very endearing. By simplicity I don't mean stupidity, but a simplicity of thinking with which one can totally relax and be free of any complexity.

We had been manoeuvred by Mother from a very early age into enjoying whatever we had to do. So that although we had some very cold, windy and tiring days pulling and tapping beet, we were in good spirits.

We had to walk about two miles to get to the farm, and we often sang and even danced on our way there. Soon the boys who had come to work with us were smitten with our lightheartedness and added their bit by bringing a mouth-organ and by telling stories and jokes, often bawdy.

Of course the working day was very short, and we made very little money, but the fact that we earned anything at all and that we had something physical to do, was very pleasing. To be without the horror of penniless idleness gave the young lads much satisfaction too. So that sometimes we were even boisterous, much to the bewilderment of the ploughman who came to lift the sugar-beet. 'What ye can get tae laugh at, wi' yer noses tae the grund an' the bloddy wind nearly liftin' ye in the air, is beyond me.' However, by the end of a week he too became quite jovial, telling us jokes and reciting Burns very expertly. We found out that reading Burns was his hobby.

So in this way we carried on until almost the beginning of a new year. January, February and March were very lean months, with nothing for us to do in the fields. Lean because of our own stupidity, if you like, because we never prepared in any way for the days ahead, nor even for the next day. Every day had to look for itself. We were quite incapable of thinking of the future in a material way.

So we were often hungry but, oh, the satisfaction we got from a meal which we had obtained by perhaps finding someone needing a chair mended, or by selling rabbit skins, or in exchange for the small-wares which Mother always kept.

We often had to walk many miles and return empty-handed too, but a day without food did not put us up nor down very much. In fact it sharpened our wits to think of something to raise the wind for the next day. Bryce, who cycled round the bothies selling to the ploughmen, sometimes came to our rescue if he had a good day, by giving Mother a few coppers.

41

One night he told me that he would like me to dress like most of the other traveller girls, and insisted that I take five shillings from him to buy a traveller's overall. Those overalls were all the rage with traveller women and girls, and were made specially for them.

They were sleeveless with a waistband and crossed over below the waist, fastened by three big buttons at each side, big horse-shoe pockets, and a slit centre back at the bottom. Older women always chose black sateen for the material; the younger ones any pretty material which they fancied, or self-coloured. A few shops here and there specialised in making clothes for travellers, and would send samples of colours available. Light ginghams were very popular for summer wear. A traveller girl was 'dressed' when she wore one of those overalls. No coat was thought necessary. The same shops made aprons and black velvet skirts for more wealthy travellers. The skirts had a deep waistband and were pleated all round from the hip-bone downwards. Men liked a silk handkerchief looped through a gold wedding ring. I chose apple-green for my overall. It fitted perfectly, and did help improve my rather boyish figure.

Bryce was delighted. He did not much fancy the knowledge that non-traveller boys sometimes tried to 'pick me up'. If they knew that I was a traveller, he thought, they would be deterred. Like most traveller men jealousy was a very strong point with him.

Come April and we got potato planting work to do. We went out in lorries belonging to the potato growers. Those lorries had no sides on them and often around thirty people sat at the back of them, some with their feet and legs dangling over the sides and back.

The cold winds seemed to go right through you as the lorry sped along. One grower had a Foden lorry which had

a chimney that belched black smoke. The black smoke flew
back on top of us making our eyes smart and covering us with
soot. What we must have looked like God alone knows.

You had to be in the field by seven o'clock in the morning when the ploughmen started their day. It was a rather
toilsome task. The blustery April winds were often choked
with showers of hail. One could hear a change in the tone
of the wind as during the showers we walked up and down
drills placing the potatoes about nine inches apart. We carried
the potatoes in an old sack with a hole cut in it to go over
our heads. A ploughman would fill it up again as soon as
it was empty. We finished at five-thirty and by the time we
got home it was dark.

Mother just would not stay at home, although Katie and
I prigged with her. 'I maun get oot o' the hoose,' she said.
When May came in, a rather sad unrest gripped her in spite
of the breath of summer on the budding trees. Father had
died the previous May.

42

One evening when Mother failed to come back after going
shopping I went to look for her.

At that time lots of pubs had tiny places near the door
with a wee hatch through which drinks could be served. We
called them booie holes. Any woman could slip into those
little places almost unnoticed.

I had read the signs with Mother. Recently she had talked
much of olden times, her girlhood, parents, her dead children
and early days with my father. I knew that her heart was
sair, and that the pain smouldering there would burst out.
Memories had filled her soul with melancholy, too strong
even for her, and came between her and the past.

I found her in one of those wee booie holes, much the
worse of drink, but her wits were still intact. Her first words
left me in no doubt of that. 'Have you been raking round

the bars looking for me, lassie? You're no' feared, with so many drunk men going about?'

At that time men often got the wrong idea if they saw a girl go into a bar, and just might follow her and become nasty. Only a certain type of girl went into bars, especially on a Saturday night.

'No, Ma. You ken fine that I wouldn't go into a bar on my own. Anyway what about yoursel'? How do you think that we feel about you? You're still a fine-looking woman, and not old yet.'

'How did you ken I would be here?' she went on. 'Did you tell Katie and the wean that you were going to look for me?'

'No, I didnae tell them,' I answered. 'I had noticed that you hae been a bit dowie lately, and I just thocht that you would fa' back on your auld freend.'

'Well just haud on a minute and I'll come hame wi' ye,' she said, tapping on the wee closed hatch as she spoke. It was so small that barely a half of the barman's face could be seen when he opened it. 'Bring me a jill if you please,' she told him. After paying for it she put the jill of whisky into the big horse-shoe pocket of her apron, and gathered her shawl round about her, saying, 'Come then, tak' me hame, bairn.'

Once home she sat and finished the whisky, singing mournful old Gaelic songs until she fell asleep. Lexy was a bit disturbed at seeing Mother so drunk. 'I'm no' sleeping wi' her this night,' she declared.

'You can sleep wi' Katie,' I told her, 'and I will sleep wi' Mother.'

'Did she no' have any messages?' Katie asked. I shook my head in answer. 'I'll bet she hasnae a penny left in her pocket either,' Katie went on. 'This carry-on is no' good enough. We could aa die wi' the hunger, for aa she cares.' Katie always was a bit more wordie when she was worried, and her real worry was about Mother, not food.

Luckily Bryce came quite early on the Sunday. 'How is the joy o' my hert this morning,' he said, sitting down beside me on the door-step.

'No' very joyful,' I answered him. 'Mother's in the dol-drums o' drink, there's neither bite nor sup in the hoose, and it's Sunday.'

'What has Sunday to do with it?' he asked.

'Well I cannae go tae the doors on a Sunday, can I?'

'Are you hungry?' he asked, putting his arm around my shoulders.

'No' really,' I said, leaning against him. 'It's just that I don't like to see Mother like that.'

'I ken how you feel,' he went on. 'My folk were heavy drinkers before my father died. My sister used to look after us when they had those bouts of drinking. I will never be a drunkard.'

Then he gave me a little squeeze and rose up, putting his hand in his pocket. 'Here, tak' this,' he said, handing me some money. 'I am going somewhere. I'll no' be lang. You get something from the wee shop for that.' He then went and jumped on his bicycle and left.

Mother was sitting with her face the colour of clay, and a bandana tied tightly round her head, Indian style. 'My head is bouncing off my body wi' the accursed drink,' she said. 'I have the bile.' Then, 'Where did Bryce go? Did he give you money for that bread and things?'

I nodded and said, 'I don't know where he went, Ma, but I'm going to toast a bit of this bread, and you can dip it in water, and try to eat it. It will break the bile. I got some aspirin too, for your headache.'

'God knows what came ower me yesterday. I just let the power o' thocht get the better o' me. Thocht can be an awful thing if it gangs in the wrang direction.'

'Ach dinnae worry, Ma. You'll be as right as rain in a wee while,' I told her.

Katie, who had been going about in silence all morning, took over the toasting and tea-making. Lexy was pleased to see it. She was a great reader and was nearly always sitting amidst a scatterment of books when she was in the house.

Mother's efforts to break the bile were partially successful and she was looking a bit brighter when Bryce came back.

'Here, Mag,' he said, handing Mother a wee musken o' whisky. 'I had to go to Edzell for that.'

At that time only a few public houses were allowed to open on Sundays. They were not permitted to sell drink to any local residents. Only to what they called 'bonafide' travellers. One had to sign a book to that effect.

'Oh, God bless you, laddie. I'll never forget you for this.' Mother was downing the neat whisky as she spoke. It is really surprising what 'a hair from the dog that bit you' can do, and soon she was much recovered.

43

Bryce had come in early because we had planned, Mother and I, to walk out to where he was camped to see his mother and other travellers. He had been pestering me to come out for weeks. 'If you take me out, I'll come,' I had told him. 'I doubt if I can come with you two,' Mother told us, 'but go wi' the laddie, Betsy, when you promised.'

Bryce was staying at a camp called Pow Soddies, about four miles out the old Forfar road, down over the old bridge and then up a path through a big wood. Birds were flittering and twittering about in ecstasy as we walked along with his arm around me. May flowers were scattered all through the wood as thick as stars in the Milky Way.

'Oh, isn't everything so beautiful?' I cried. 'Come on, let's go into the wood a bit, we might find a bird's nest.'

Soon we were sitting kissing, surrounded with the delights of nature in spring. I snuggled very close to him, but suddenly he said, whilst gently pushing me away, 'Lassie, you don't know what you are doing to me.'

His words were true. I was as yet unawakened, and completely ignorant of the ways of a man's sensuality. So I was a bit peeved and said, 'Do you no' like kissing me?'

'I like it too much,' he told me, getting up and proffering me a hand.

I could not see the logic of his last remark, and when he put his arm round me again, I pushed it off, saying, 'Now see how you like it.'

'Oh, lassie, it's a good job that it's me you're with and not some other man.' He strode away in front of me as he said this. I turned at that and had every intention of going back home, but the rattle of an old bicycle made me turn around again.

One of Bryce's young nephews was riding it. He was a bit younger than me. 'Your mother is wondering what's keeping you,' he shouted, jumping off the bike. 'She expected you about dinner time.'

Bryce came back to where I stood and held out his hand to me, saying, 'Coming?' I was on the point of saying no before I looked up into his brown eyes with the glisk of love in them.

His mother was a little dark woman who had lived with her three sons since her husband had died some years before. She had had ten children, and two of her married daughters were camped near her. She had a slight fear that because I was living in a house and therefore could keep myself a bit cleaner, I would perhaps be a bit difficult. I soon put her at her ease on that score.

She had host of wee grand-bairns all specially cleaned up for my coming. They gradually crept closer and closer, till there were two on my knees, and others trying to take their places by shoving them off. Their mothers hastened to reprove them, but I told them to let the bairns be.

Bryce's two brothers had both of us blushing with their snide banter and teasing. All of them showed a genuine delight at meeting me, and gave me a pair of gold earrings, a ring and a brooch which I knew very well were treasures of their own hearts. Yet not to have taken their presents would have hurt them more than parting with them.

Bryce took me home. He was jubilant because his people liked me and sang as we almost skipped along. He had a beautiful voice. I too sang, not as beautifully but just as cheerfully.

After a while I told him that I would be writing to my cousin

Johnnie to ask him if he could find a place for us to work at the turnip singling. 'I must get Mother away from the house for a while,' I told him. 'She is weary of the restricting walls.'

'Then you will be miles away from me.' He didn't sound very pleased about that.

'I'll write to you,' I told him.

'Betsy,' he went on, 'I have seen a few of your cousins when we were up at the berry-picking at Blair. There are some really handsome fellows among them. Will you go out with any of them if they ask you?'

'Why do you ask?' I countered him.

'Oh, Betsy, you know how I feel about you. I just can't bear the thocht, even. I wish you wouldn't go. The thocht o' you wi' somebody else drives me crazy.' He was getting all het up now. 'Promise that you won't.'

'For God's sake man, what's the matter with you? Are you bothered with jealousy?' I laughed as I said this.

'Yes, yes, I am a jealous person. It's no' funny, Betsy. Don't laugh.' He gripped my shoulders tightly as he spoke and there were tears in the eyes that I looked up at. I shrugged my shoulders to let him know that his grip hurt. 'Oh, I'm sorry,' he said, letting go of me.

'You are eating yourself with jealousy,' I told him. 'Eating your own heart. That's not love, Bryce. It's madness, and furthermore it's a great insult to me. If it makes you any happier then I will promise not to let any fellow within yards of me. Happy now?'

'If you mean it, yes, I am happy,' but his looks belied his words. He still looked a bit troubled. I felt a wee twinge of uneasiness myself. Was he going to be too possessive, I wondered.

 44

A few days later I got a reply from cousin Johnnie who was Uncle Andy's, my father's brother's, son. I did not want to go to the Highlands where Mother's relations lived. They were darling people but rather fond of John Barleycorn. Johnnie said that he would be down for us on Saturday. 'Thank God,' Mother said, 'I'm truly weary o' this house.'

Mother was not the only one weary of the house. Poor wee Ricky was like a prisoner in it. We had received a letter from the Council saying that they had been told that we were keeping a dog. I could only take him out at night. Sometimes I got up at four o'clock in the morning to let him get some exercise. Bryce came every evening since he knew that we were going away. Friday night he showed his reluctance to go home. 'You will keep that promise?' he asked.

'That seems to be more important to you than the fact that we will be separated,' I answered. 'I must be free, Bryce. I can't bear to be restricted too much.'

'I won't restrict you from doing anything else. Anything except going out with another fellow. Of course I will miss you. Mind and write care of the post office. I love you, Betsy.' He had never said this before, and I knew that he had difficulty getting it out. 'I wish I could just tak you hame wi' me.'

'Some day,' I answered, 'if you be a good boy. Goodnight now. I'm getting cold.' We had been standing for about an hour outside the door of the house and I am sure for another hour at the gate.

Katie had been busy bundling up our bits and pieces, and cleaning everything in the house almost. 'You are a great help, Peesie,' she burst out as soon as I came in. She called me Peesie when she was annoyed with me. 'You'll no' rax yoursel' very much, will ye?'

I very much wanted the glow of Bryce's 'I love you, Betsy' to bide with me, and I got very irritated with Katie's remarks. Even though I knew that she had good reason for them. Her next words really knocked everything but wild anger from my mind. 'Dinnae tell me that you could be doing any good out there with a man all this time,' she said. I could feel all control ebbing out of me. So I made out towards the door, only to be grabbed by Mother who had been in a bedroom.

'Let me out, Ma,' I said. 'Let me out or I'll make her face like a cow's cunt.'

Mother was really shocked. 'Lassie, dear. Your father will turn in his grave.' On this the tears came and I ran and got into bed.

Lexy came into bed beside me that night. Katie slept with Mother. 'I love you, Betsy,' Lexy whispered. 'Dinnae greet.' Then she put her arm round my waist.

'Tell me a story,' she went on. The one about the silly woman.'

'That's a wean's story,' I answered.

'But I like that one,' she insisted. Soon we were both giggling. Her giggles made me giggle too, as I related the tale to her.

Strangely enough, I slept long and soundly that night. Believe it or not, Katie came and wakened me. The others were all up. 'Do you want a cup o' tea?' she asked. 'Or would you rather make my face like a cow's . . .?' We nearly spilled the tea as we both shook with laughter.

Cousin Johnnie was in high spirits when he arrived at mid-day. 'Wait till you see the darling camping place,' he told us. 'Tons o' sticks and a wee burn wi' ice-cold water right beside us, and we have pitched our tents in amongst the broom, Maggie.' He planted a kiss on Mother's cheek as he said this. 'It's on an estate between Perth and Dunkeld. There's a big moor for the weans to run free in. Miles away from everybody except the estate workers. You'll love it, Maggie. The neeps, too, are perfect. Not a blade o' grass amongst them. Hardly even a weed.'

Johnnie's description of the camp was accurate, but he had failed to mention what I liked best. The banks of the burn were arrayed right along each side with all manner of wild plant life as well as trees and bushes. The wild thorn was already dressed in its braws, and filling the air with its secret perfume. Secret because no man-made perfume could possibly match it. The souch of the burn, and the mating nesting birds, mingling with the fragrance of the awakening flowers and blossoms, almost stopped my heart. Could Heaven be more pleasant?

I wondered. Ricky stood at my feet as I surveyed all this. My feelings and thoughts must surely have somehow linked into his, judging from his almost human sounds of ecstatic pleasure. 'Aye, my darlin' wee cratur, you are free again,' I said, fondling his ears.

Uncle Andy had a bantam hen which had sat clocking two goose's eggs, and was now endeavouring to mother her strange wee brood. Her defensive attitude towards Ricky was comical to see. Then I thought of Bryce. Was my yearning for him to be here only a desire for someone to share the delights of nature with? I knew that he did revel in her beauty. Or did I want him for himself? At that time I was not sure.

There was the usual set of weans in the encampment, surrounded by loving aunts, uncles, cousins, grannies and grandads, who all took an interest in their welfare. The young mothers were very tolerant of the rebukes of any of those relations. A shout of 'Hey young woman, look where your bairn is. Instead o' sitting there claiking, you should be paying more attention to your bairn.' Or 'Lassie, your bairn's gaen tae fa' into the water. If you were my wife, I'd gie ye a good hard kick in the shuch.' Shouts like that could be heard at any hour of the day, and the mothers knew that they were given because of the love for the children. They would answer back cheekily sometimes, but immediately rush to the child.

My aunts were just the tonic that Mother needed. They talked, laughed and sang as they worked, and after work. The aunts praised the looks of Katie and Lexy, then Aunt Nancy said, 'Aye, but Betsy is blossoming out a bit now too. She was a gey scranny, peeked-lookin' wee thing for a long time, but there's promise there noo.'

'She is comin' oot o' her buckie, tae,' Mother answered. 'If you had heard what she said tae me the other night, when Katie and her were arguing.' Then Mother told them what I had said.

'Ach, what ither can you expect? The weans hear that at ony hour o' the day, when they are oot in the fields.' Aunt Nancy won my heart with that remark.

'She's no' a wean noo,' Mother said.

Of course I had heard that word and many more swear words. They were thrown around at horses, dogs, and at each other by the majority of farm-workers every day. Travellers themselves were very prone to use them too. Father had drawn the line on 'taking the Saviour's name in vain,' as he put it. Other forms of swearing were just words. Yet the cant name for Jesus—Jaymity—was often sounded, and heard without any reproof. How silly can people be? As if it was any the less a sin, if spoken in cant!

Although it was late May the weather turned very disagreeable with heavy rain lashing down, and high winds howling eerie songs through the trees, leaving the hawthorn bereft of its blossom. Then on the third day about noon the sun came out so hotly that the earth was steaming. The ground between the tents was all a mass of mud, with our running from tent to tent. So we decided to shift a bit to untrodden ground. When this was done, the beds were made with fresh straw.

We had no gailies or barricades built, only summer tents with no inside place for a fire. Can you imagine standing outside in the pouring rain trying to get wet sticks alight for a fire? Some of the dry straw from our beds was used to get the fire started. Women usually did this, then did the cooking with an old sack or something over their heads and shoulders. Often women would wade through wet grass and undergrowth to gather a burden of sticks and carry them back to the camp on their backs.

Meanwhile the men would be telling stories, or playing games with the young children to keep them inside, out of the rain. Men and boys were the VIPs amongst travelling people. First their mothers and sisters, then their wives and daughters, treated them with the greatest respect and protected them most unselfishly from anything that might hurt them or damage their health. Women indeed were tougher in endurance, and took great pride in looking after their menfolk. Of course lots of men would go for the sticks, but that was about the extent of their help on the domestic side.

During the rain I had spent some time writing a letter to Bryce and reading a Bible, mostly because it was the only thing on the camp to read. Nearly every traveller family carried a Bible even though many of them could not read.

'Ma, when you are in the town for your messages will you post this letter for me?' I asked Mother. Cousin Johnnie usually drove the women to the town.

'Wha are ye writing tae? That laddie?' she asked. 'You're gettin gey thrang the two o' ye. I hope ye ken what yer daein'.' She was sitting combing her very long thick hair and plaiting it. It was the colour of ripe hazelnuts. 'There's young Duncan there. He cannae tak his een aff ye,' she went on. 'Whar could ye get a better-lookin' laddie?' Young Duncan was a cousin, and indeed a handsome fellow. 'I'm no' sayin' onything against Bryce,' Mother continued, 'but you'll no' get much shelter ahint a laich dyke.'

'Maybe no, Ma,' I answered, 'but a laich dyke is easy louped.'

'And that's the kind o' man that ye want?' Mother's voice was full of scorn. 'A man that ye can easy get the better o'? I wadnae count that a man.'

'Ma, I couldnae stand tae be snooled and trooshed wi' ony man. You ken what like aa our breed o' folk are. I like tae gang my ain way. I've nae intention o' spending my life in attendance tae ony man.'

'God help the man that gets ye,' Mother answered. 'That's aa I can say aboot ye.'

I knew that because of inbreeding most of our breed lived rather recklessly. We, including myself, were rather turbulent and unruly, and when two such people clash, need I say more?

'What aboot your bairns?' Mother was not finished with me yet.

'Ma, look at Bella's bairns. She is as happy as the day is lang.' Bella was my oldest sister who had married an outsider.

Katie, who seldom agreed with me, then spoke up and declared that she would never marry a cousin either. 'Well, well,' Mother finished up, saying 'Wha ever lives the langest will see the maist.'

45

The day was beautiful now after the rain, and the many scents rising from the drying earth mingled in the air. The wee burn, although swollen, bickered along singing praises to the welcome sun.

Lexy and about six other youngsters were playing a game of rounders. Some of them slithered to the posts on their bums as they strived to reach them before being knocked out. Pride filled me as I watched Lexy, and my heart must have sent out waves of the almost fierce love which I felt towards her. Where has my baby sister gone? I thought, as I watched the rise and fall of her breasts as she came running towards me.

'Betsy, would you please ask cousin Johnnie to take us into Perth tomorrow?' By 'us' she probably meant all the youngsters over five on the camp. 'The best picture in the world is on,' she continued. 'Its called *The Wizard of Oz*, and there's a matinee tomorrow.'

'Saturday or not, we will have to work tomorrow,' I told her, 'or the neeps will get too high, and twice as hard to do.' Then, unable to bear the look of disappointment in her lovely eyes, I said, 'Tell you what, I will ask him to take us at night. I would like to see this picture too.'

'Oh goody, goody!' she cried, jumping up and down.

Almost every night poor cousin Johnnie obligingly took a van load of people into Perth to let them go to the pictures. He usually visited friends whilst he waited to take them home again.

Uncle Andy and my other two uncles, Davie and Duncan, asked if they could take Ricky for a walk. Other relatives of ours were staying at a farm about four miles away, and they were going to see them. There were six other girls in the encampment but they were in their twenties and seemed to have their special friends amongst themselves. Katie had been admitted to their gang as it were, but somehow I just didn't fit in. Not that they deliberately ignored me, nor were unkind in any way. I just somehow felt like an intruder. So I wandered away on my own again. As yet I had not had time to explore much.

The moor was large and stretched right down to the main road. A cart track served as a road through it to the fields and farm, also to the big house. Of course there were gates and a tree-lined driveway up to the mansion house. All around the moor was almost covered with whin bushes in full bloom. Briar trees were beginning to get clad with their spring braws. Rowans, catkin trees and many other forms of plant life were just awakening. The scent of all of them was very pleasant, but for me there was nothing to beat the whins. I can't believe that there is any plant anywhere in the world that is more pleasant to one's sense of smell. I was filled with the bliss of living amongst such pleasing surroundings.

46

My mind slipped away as it was wont to. Where I do not know, so that a sound quite near made my heart jump. A man was only yards away walking on the cart road, which was a mass of gutters. What fool can this be? I thought. Fool he must be to walk there. Expensive tweed knickerbockers above what had been highly polished brown boots, and a jacket to match the trousers, told me that he was no farm worker. He was coming towards me and would pass within a few yards of where I stood dry foot on the grass.

He was carrying a thick, heavy, walking stick and I wondered if I should bolt away. However, having great faith in my running ability, I stood my ground and prepared myself to answer his greeting if he gave one. Or even to greet him first. So I looked up into eyes that looked like two wee misty lochs, and realised that they were unseeing, although he was not blind.

I was a bit frightened now, and took to my heels towards the tents but turned on hearing a thud, and there he was lying face down in the mud.

Walking back rather cautiously to within a few yards of him, I could see that his mouth and nose were right in the thick glaur. I could hear his breath hissing. He will suffocate, I thought. His staff was lying near him, where it had dropped out of his hand. I picked it up and prodded his shoulders with it. Then I gave him a sharp tap on the knuckles, but he didn't move.

He is really dead out, poor soul, I was thinking as I pulled his head sideways. Sure enough, his eyes, nostrils, and mouth were all full of mud. I tried to pull the tail of his jacket up to wipe them but he was a heavy man. The grass was short and useless too, so I darted behind a whin bush and pulled off my white cotton knickers and cleared his nostrils with them. Then his mouth and eyes. The mud had not really gotten inside his mouth, because his teeth were tightly clenched. His breathing reminded me of a bull blowing. He's dying, I thought, and took off like a hare to get help.

I got to the tent completely out of breath and shaking with fear. Between gasps I managed to say, 'Man!' and point across to where he was lying, but of course he could not be seen from there. Still gasping for breath I could only shake my head vigorously when Mother shouted, 'My God! Some man has been at my bairn!'

Then I realised that the muddy knickers were still in my hand and that I was practically covered with mud myself. Mother had jumped to the obvious conclusion, and before I was able to enlighten her, five young men were going like deer towards where I had pointed, leaping over whin bushes and tree stumps, as they went. I made to run after them thinking, They'll kill him! but Mother came after me, grabbed me by the hair and came a scud off my ear, uttering a torrent of rebukes. So I ran into the tent sobbing.

Mother came in after me still ranting. 'How often have I warned you about going off on your own like that? No better could happen to you.'

Having regained my breath I said, 'Nothing has happened to me, Ma. They have gone after a poor sick man. I was going to stop them.' Then I told her what had happened. 'Stop them, Ma!' I sobbed.

Almost the whole encampment were making their way across the moor. Women, girls, and children, going much more leisurely after the young men.

'If they harm onybody it will be aa your fault. I'll wheeple tae them.' Mother put her forefinger and thumb together at the points, then whistled through them several times. The sound was very loud and pierced the air in all directions. Five short blasts, and one long, higher-pitched. A warning whistle. 'If they dinnae hear that they must be deaf.'

Mother was visibly shaken by the fear that I had given her. That is why she had hit me. She was like many of my relations, a bit like a peat fire. Apparently just a cold heap of ash and sods, but smouldering red hot in the heart. Mother's whistle had brought most of the women and children back, also Katie and the other girls. They laughed uproariously when Mother related to them what I had told her.

Then Aunt Nancy said, 'Dinnae worry, Maggie, the laddies are no' fools. They'll no' touch the cratur o' a man.' Then, looking straight at me, continued, 'That's a bad habit ye have going off like that on yer own. If ye were mine I'd soon put that oot o' ye, my lass.' I didn't answer her back. 'It's as well that your Uncle Andy is no' here, or your legs would be feeling the sting o' his steel-lined whip, and weel ye deserve it.'

Aunt Nancy was Mother's only sister, and her word was law with her own family. Even her married son wouldn't turn the word with her. 'Would any young woman worry her mother like that?' She kept on at me until I felt that I had committed the most heinous crime.

The boys seemed to take a long time before returning and we were all a bit apprehensive what might have happened. However, as Aunt Nancy had said, they were not fools. On their return all were eager to tell us. 'Let Johnnie speak,' Mother asked. Johnnie was the oldest.

'It was the laird himself,' Johnnie told us. 'I kent that he

was in an epileptic fit, the minute that I clapped eyes on him.'
Then to me, 'It's as weel, lassie, that you cam' hame. It took
the five o' us tae haud him. He would have spawled us to
bits. Poor dear man, and to think that only this mornin' I
was envying him. It just goes to show ye.'

Here young Duncan butted in. 'I was nearly gaen tae hit
him wi' his ain cromack,' he said, 'with the fricht o' my ain
body, when he came at me like a raging bull.' Here the others
all started to laugh and tease him about his lack of bravery.
'A dead brave man is no' much use tae himsel' nor onybody
clse,' Duncan defended himself.

'How-an-ever,' Johnnie continued, 'twa o' us ran tae the
big hoose, and his wife took us wi' her in a car back to where
he was lying. He quietened doon and just lay staring, after a
while. His wife telt us that he used tae drive an aeroplane,
and that he was nearly burned tae death when it crashed wi'
him. She says that ye could hardly put a pin-point doon on
his body whar there is nae mark o' burns. She thinks that
that must have brought on they fits that he taks.'

For the rest of the evening there was much talk about the
incident.

47

I was making the last tea of the day when Ricky bounded up
to me. On looking round my heart gave a dunt and nearly
jumped out of my mouth when I saw who was coming with
my uncles. A raven black head and a bright red one were
visible now and then above the broom bushes.

I put the tea-can down and ran with Ricky at my heels
towards them. 'Betsy!' Annie of the raven hair shouted, and
ran towards me. Jessie, however, beat her to it and knocked
me over in the impact. Annie threw herself on top of both
of us, and we rolled and clung in the ecstatic delight of
seeing each other again. I had not seen Annie since Daddy's
funeral.

She was no blood relation, in fact she was not a traveller. My Uncle Jimmie had married her mother after she had been thrown out by her father because she was pregnant. So Annie was really Uncle Jimmie's stepdaughter. It was rare to rear a stepchild, but these were rare circumstances. Uncle Jimmie adored his wife's beautiful child, and because of her black hair and dark skin, he used to call her his 'wee cluster o' nuts'. Jessie of course had been with us at the tattie picking.

'We have been so close to you, and didn't know that you were here,' Jessie said.

'We're shifting ower here this very night,' Annie told me. 'That farmer we were working for is a pure guffie. He has been charging us a sixpence for a thimble-full o' skimmed milk, and a shillin' for a handful o' hay for the ponies. He wouldnae let the wee weans intae the neep-field, in case they tramped on his neeps. Aunt Jean had tae look after the weans at the camp.'

Jessie took up the story from there. 'Aye,' she said, 'but wait till ye hear what he did the nicht, when we were comin' here. He was standin' wi' twa ither farmers beside the farm. They were aa well smeeked wi' drink. "Wha the hell are you lot?" he roared. "You dinnae work for me. So get tae blazes aff my property, and dinnae let me see ye back here again. Dirty tink bastards."

'Now ye ken what like Uncle Davy gets if anybody ca's him a bastard.

' "Stall, man," Uncle Andy told him.

' "No! I'll no' stall," Davy replied. "I'm no' lettin' that lantern-jawed man ca' me a bastard." Then he shouted tae the farmer, "No mister! My mother never reared ony bastards. If there is ony bastard here, it's yersel."

' "Oh shaness, Uncle!" I warned Davie, but he was too wild to heed me.

' "I'll stand sixty days in Perth prison for him. I'll gie him a bastard's mark that he will carry wi' him to the grave."

'Then he made a darry at the farmer. Ah, but the farmer wasnae gaen tae face up tae him. He ran and let this wild collie dog off the chain. Now this dog is as ill-natured as the man

himself, and ferocious. It's a good job Uncle Andy was there.'
Here Jessie started to laugh, and said, 'That's a brave wee dog,
your Ricky. He jumped up into my arms wi' the fright. Didn't
you, ye wee coward?' She stroked Ricky's ears as she spoke.

'Anyway,' she continued, 'As I was telling you, if Uncle
Andy hadnae been there the farmer's dog would have torn
us to pieces. He only spoke canny tae it, but it stopped in its
tracks. Then went doon on its belly, and crawled up to Uncle
Andy, and started to lick the back o' his hand. It completely
ignored the farmer shouting at it to bite us.

'Well, if you could have seen they farmers' faces! I never
saw men sobering up so quickly in my life. One of them
walked over to Uncle Andy and put his hand out. "Man,
that's the best I've ever seen. Shake! I'll bet ye are real good
wi' young colts."

'"I can handle any animal," Andy told him, "but I can
dae very little wi' some men."

'"That's what they ca' The Horseman's Word, isn't it?"
the man went on.

'"I couldnae tell ye what it's ca'ed, mister. It just comes
naturally tae me."

'The anger had left Uncle Davie, and he never attempted
again tae hit the farmer. Then Uncle Andy looked at the
owner of the dog and said, "I am sorry for that poor animal.
Cry him back and chain him. You are the one who should
really be in chains, and if ye want the rest o' your neeps done,
you had better look for other workers. I was doon lookin' at
and measuring what my brothers have done, and I will thank
you to give me their coppers. They have done four acre and
you had better pay them for four acre."

'"To hell wi' you," the farmer said, "They'll get bugger
all frae me."

'"Do ye want me tae mak' yer ain dog spawl ye in bits?"

'The man hesitated, then went intae the hoose and come
oot wi' some money in his hand. When Andy looked at it
he said, "Come, come, noo, mister. I can coont, ye ken. I
think tuppence-halfpenny a hundred yards is cheap enough
without cheatin'."

'Well onyway,' Jessie went on, 'tae mak' a lang story short and a short story lang, Uncle Andy got what we were entitled tae. Then we went back tae the camp and gave it to them. They are aa shiftin' ower here. They shouldnae be lang till they come.'

When we got to the camp my uncles were busy telling all the rest what had happened. Mother was delighted that Aunt Jean was coming, and I was absolutely in my element at having Annie and Jessie.

48

Two days after that the laird and his lady visited us in the evening. At their approach the noisy uproar of the camp ceased, and everyone began to lift anything that was lying about, to make the place tidier. Some even ran inside the tents to hide, so that only a small group were standing around the fire when the gentry got there.

'Good evening,' the laird greeted them. 'I have come down to thank you for your assistance the other evening. I am very grateful.'

'Yes I could never have managed without you,' his wife added.

'I believe that it was a young lady who found me,' the laird went on, 'Could I see her, please?'

'Surely, sir,' Mother answered, then shouted my name. I emerged from behind the broom bushes, with Annie and Jessie at my heels.

'My goodness!' the lady said. 'A redhead, a blonde, and a brunette.'

Jessie pushed me forward saying, 'It was the blonde who saved your life, sir.'

'Saved my life?' he repeated.

Jessie had assumed that the boys had told the lady about my lifting his face clear of the mud.

I looked up at him. The grey eyes were not misty now, but

very clear and inquisitive. 'You were face down in the mud, sir,' I answered his enquiring eyes. 'I just turned your head a little.'

'Then you probably did save my life.' Then looking all around he added. 'Is there nowhere to sit down here?'

Cousin Johnnie speedily pulled two wicker chairs out of his van. Aunt Jean just as speedily wiped the seats of them and proffered one to the lady. They both sat down, apparently quite at ease, and conversed with my aunts and uncles. Some of the children gradually came out of the bushes or other hiding places and stood around in respectful silence. The adults did likewise until there was quite a crowd listening to the laird's tales of his travels and his accident. He was one of the kind of talkers that laughs himself and makes others laugh at things which must have caused him heavy sorrow.

The fire had failed to reach his face which was a blessing, as he was a very attractive man, big with dark curly hair. His wife was less striking but had that air of breeding which cannot be disguised. She talked to the bairns mostly. 'Well,' the laird said, 'I know how I can reward the young lady, but what about the young men? Is there any way that I can do that?' They both rose as he spoke.

Uncle Andy spoke for them all. He was the sort of man born to lead. 'They want nothing, sir. We are all more than sorry that you ever needed any help.'

'Yes,' the laird answered, 'but there must be something.'

'Well, there is one thing that we would very much appreciate, sir. As ye ken it is very hard to get anywhere to camp nowadays, and I can see mysel' stuck in the hoose all summer before mony years gang ower my head. If I could come here for a day or twa even—we wouldn't bother anybody. Just to get away from the tea-box wi' bricks around it.'

'Then you must be one of those lucky people who have been given a new council house?' The laird laughed as he spoke.

'Lucky, did you say? It is the worst thing that ever happened tae me in my lifetime. I had a darlin' wee hoose, wi' a big back green, and a wash-hoose, and sheds. I could plouter aboot there and keep an animal, and nobody ever bothered me. I could saw sticks and keep a puckle rags and rabbit-skins in the winter. Noo I can get daen nothing but pacing up and doon inside that tea-box. If I lose the head some day and give it a hard kick, I am sure it will fa' doon aboot me. And I'm telling ye, man. Some days I'd like tae fie it a twa or three good hard kicks and makin' it intae spin-drift! In the name o' God how can folk live like that? Every natural impulse has tae be curbed. Ye daurnae sing. Ye daurnae play yer pipes nor yer box. Ye cannae even gie a loud laugh but ye are disturbing somebody.

'Nae wonder what it says in that blessed book that's lyin' below my head there. The wean read it oot tae me the ither day. "Woe to them that build hoose tae hoose, and set field tae field," it says. So that there is nae place in the world whaur ye can dae what ye want. Well that's what it meant onyway. Woe it says, and woe is the right word for that way o' livin'. That's the truest words that were ever said.

'Then if I leave the hoose and gang tae look for some place tae put up my tent, I am gaered pull it doon again before the day is oot. What are folk gaen tae dae? Sit in their wee square holes like a moose that's been chased wi' a pussy cat? Feared to tae mak' a meek. Nae fun o' ony kind? Naething but eat, work, and sleep, and shake wi' the fright in case you are breathing too loud!'

Uncle Andy had completely forgotten who he was talking to. His face was as red as the embers of the fire. He had worked himself up into a state verging on hysteria, with the power of his own thoughts. Most of the weans and young folk had dispersed into hiding again, after repeated mutterings of 'Shaness! shaness!' had been ignored.

Then suddenly he seemed to realise that he was more than a bit carried away, and looked very embarrassed. 'Ach, dinnae heed me, laird. I'm just an auld blether. I'm sorry, I shouldnae be speakin' like that tae a man in your position. A landed gentleman.'

The laird's grey eyes were twinkling, as were the blue ones

of his wife. I am sure that they were both silently amused at Uncle's outburst. 'You too, are just as much a man, Andy, but I am a bit confused about what you're getting so fired up about.'

'Well, you see sir, it's like this. For lang and lang folk like us, tinkers, travellers, or whatever you like tae ca' us, have moved aboot through the country. We could bide on ony bit o' common land, living the way that we like to. We keep tae oorsels and try as much as possible tae bother, or be a nuisance tae, naebody. Nowadays, however, we have mostly tae depend on farmers who need us to work in the fields or on gentlemen like yourself to give us a bit of land to stay on.

'Of course when the work is finished, we are expected tae move on. So we bundle up and take to the road, intending to stay for a night or two on one o' these pieces o' common land. But what happens? Fences, barbed-wire fences, to keep us out and No Camping signs put up. And the same thing is happening all ower the country.

'Lucky, did you say, to get a new council house? Oh, man, man, if only you could guess the agonies o' it! A cat forced tae swim across a wide water would be happier than I am in that hoose. Now dinnae get me wrang. I appreciate what the authorities are trying tae dae, but I cannae get daein' a thing. I cannae gang out wi' my pony gathering rags or scrap or whatever. There's nae place tae keep a pony! Aa the auld stables are being pulled doon. Nae place tae keep anything. Just the fower square waa's o' the hoose.'

The laird, who had been standing looking down at my uncle, gave a quick smile and said, 'Well, well, when you put it that way how can I refuse you? If you had been spokesman for Edward, I am sure he still would have been King.'

This immediately brought Andy back to his sense. 'Ach, dinnae heed me, laird. I'm just an auld blether. A God's idiot, that's what I am.'

'You are not that, Andrew, and I meant what I said. You can come here and play your pipes or whatever takes your fancy. We'll maybe even come along and hooch to you.'

He was smiling again. 'We must away now,' he continued, taking his wife by the arm. She had stood silently listening with mixed expressions. Whatever reward they had meant to give me was evidently forgotten.

49

Mother and Aunt Jean were asked to stay at the camp to cook for all the crowd. It was mostly large iron pots of rabbit stew or broth, served with oaten bannocks, or stoved tatties and skirlie.

Anyway, the following evening when we came home from the field, Mother told me that the lady of the big house had been down with her car. 'Wait till you see the barry tuggery that she brought for you.'

'I cannae wait, Ma. Let me see them now,' I asked.

Jessie and Annie too cried, 'Aye! let us see them, Aunt Maggie!'

Soon all the young women on the camp were gathered round several big cardboard boxes filled with the loveliest clothes imaginable. There was much grabbing and whoops of delight as yet another fine garment was pulled out. 'Oh, look at this!' 'Oh, look at that!' came from all directions. The clothes had belonged to the laird's three daughters who were away at school.

In the end they all got something. I settled for a voile dress with a full skirt and a little cape at the back. Annie was holding tightly on to a blue taffeta one with a pink cloth rose on the shoulder.

Jessie, never really fussy about clothes, had put on a hat with ostrich feathers, and a fox fur round her neck. Imitating the deep cultured voice of the lady herself, she strutted up to cousin Duncan and said, with appropriate gestures, 'Home, James, and don't spare the horses.'

'Are we going to get a bite to eat the night?' was his reply, 'God knows you are ugly enough without putting that on.'

Then minutes later Annie emerged from their tent with the blue taffeta on, and she was breathtaking in spite of her bare feet.

No-one ever dreamed of saying, 'Can I have this?' or 'Can I have that?' Had I protested they would have been astonished and very hurt. Sharing was the done thing. Lexy, my cute young sister, however, had somehow managed to smuggle a good sized bundle into our tent and later took them from their hiding place. 'They are for you and me, Betsy,' she said.

'You fly wee imp!' I cuddled her as I spoke.

Later Katie let us see her in a dark green knitted suit.

'That must have belonged to the lady herself,' Mother said then added, 'If ye had the price o' aa that claes ye wouldnae need tae want aa winter.'

Of course I had thought about Bryce quite often during that time. I had also received two letters from him. He expressed his feelings quite openly in simple, often mis-spelled, words. His schooling had been rather limited. Haughty pride would have prevented most traveller men from writing in this open-hearted manner, lest they should lower themselves to a mere female. Bryce's letters endeared him all the more to me. He was without that kind of pride.

With there being so many of us the work was soon finished. The laird and the farmer both thanked us for doing it so speedily and skilfully. 'You don't need to shift until you want to,' the farmer told us, but Uncle Jimmie—Annie's father—and Uncle Davie decided to take a chance on the road. 'We are wearying for the hills and glens. Surely we will find a wee patch o' ground here and there to camp on.'

Uncle Davie was the most restless wanderer amongst my father's brothers. 'Anyway,' he continued, 'Bella needs to see her ain folk sometime.' Bella, Davie's wife, came from Argyllshire. She was a Reid.

Andy and Duncan and Willie, all uncles too, said that they were staying. 'We are gaen tae pearl-fish for a while,' Uncle Duncan, the most easy-going one, said. 'We are no' aa that far fae the Tay here, and you couldnae get a better spot tae bide. Johnnie is gaen tae run us men tae the Big Burn every day. The women can dae what they like.'

Then he asked Mother and Aunt Jean what they wanted to do. 'We're quite happy here,' Mother answered for them both. 'In fact I am that pleased tae get away fae the hoose, I would bide ony place.'

Annie prigged to get staying with us but her mother would not allow her. Because she was Uncle Jimmie's stepdaughter he would not go against what his wife decided. Jessie and I would miss her terribly. We had spent rapturous days together, and pleasant evenings. Exchanging day-dreams, and talking of the things nearest our hearts, as girls will. Annie and I had rejected any advances made by our cousins, in much the same way. A quiet pretence of being ignorant of their feelings deterred them, without us having to say a word. Jessie, however, responded to young Johnnie. They eventually married, but not before much water had flowed under the bridge, as they say.

The weather turned out to be ideal for pearl fishing. Often the ponies were yoked early in the morning and the whole encampment went to spend the balmy summer days on the banks of the Big Burn. Bairns and the very young frolicked about in and out of the water, under the sharp, attentive eyes of teenagers and older ones. Those raptured days sped and June was welcoming July before we even noticed.

Luck too was with the fishers. Several fair-sized pearls had been found. So they decided to sell them and have a week or two just going from camp to camp, meeting and enjoying the company of other travellers, until the berry-picking started.

Jessie and I both loved nature, and our willing souls had been more often carried away on the wings of fledglings, butterflies and dragonflies, than in our possessions.

The company of my aunts had done wonders for Mother. They had been going out together to sell baskets, heather pot-scrubbers and smallware, whilst the men fished for pearls. The young men had found one or two farmers who needed their drystone dykes repaired. Jessie and I had carried large buckets of water for more than half a mile to fill up a draw-well for an old couple. The well had gone dry. Work was play to our young minds and bodies. We sang and capered as we did it. Payment was mostly in the form of food— usually eggs, jam or milk.

Most travellers liked to sell their pearls to a Perth jeweller named Cairncross, and would come from far and near to do business with him. He never took advantage of them but dealt fairly, even with the most humble and needy, who often would have settled for much less. He would also let them have gold earrings and rings for their wives and daughters at the lowest price possible. Probably before their next visit to Cairncross those rings and earrings would have been given away, but the men never said, 'I am buying you no more.' Sometimes the men would get a gold lever watch and chain for themselves if they found a few good pearls. They, too, didn't keep them for long.

Anyway, we travelled around Fife and Perthshire, stopping at any camping place still open, or at farms where other travellers were staying.

The men played their pipes, boxes and fiddles, and exchanged horses or complete yokes. They also liked to see the children as they grew up, and above all they loved to talk to each other, as did the women. Sometimes they sat cracking till the birds gave their early morning concert.

Soon the pearl-money ran out and it is possible that, had my uncles kept on at the fishing, they would have had, with luck, a good bit of money. However the chance to visit friends and relations was more important to them.

So we arrived back at Blairgowrie anxious to get started to pick the berries. When we got to Lethendy, where we had decided to stay, the farmer told us that he was no longer allowed to let us camp anywhere except in the field where all the other pickers were. This field was covered with bell-tents, ropes to ropes.

'I have had to provide toilet facilities and a place for them to wash themselves in.' He already had a very big hotplate, with a large boiler full of hot water always available. The toilets consisted of four dry lavatories, and a huge horses' trough provided the washing facilities.

The farmer was as disappointed as we were about the whole thing. 'Would ye no' consider biding there?' he asked. 'They are maistly Glesca folk and I never hae ony bother wi' them.'

'No, mister, wi' the help o' God. You couldnae gie me a hundred pound a day tae bide there. I'm no' sayin' that there is onything wrang wi' the folk, but that's nae use tae our kind.'

So they found a place at a farm which only had a few acres of fruit and needed no more than ourselves and their locals. No-one had as yet bothered the farmer about facilities. Most of the young folk were very disappointed as we were not allowed to go into Blairgowrie at night, men excepted of course. We also missed the lively humour and singing which we would have heard at Lethendy.

50

One night after returning from Blair, cousin Johnnie told us that he had met a young fellow who was asking for us.

'We were standing at the Wellmeadow watching the antics of aa the different folk, and he came ower and said, "Are you a Townsley?"

'"Aye," says I.

'"Would you happen to ken whaur a woman ca'ed Maggie Townsley is bidin'?" he asked.

'"No' me," I told him.

'"This woman has three lassies and bides in Brechin," he went on, but I never made him ony the wiser. His name was Whyte.'

I had never let on to anyone about Bryce and neither had Mother. 'Oh, I think I ken wha' you mean,' she answered Johnnie. 'There is a lot o' Whytes doon that way.'

However, I was to see Bryce sooner than I expected. We

went back to Brechin just after the berry-picking finished that year, and on the way home in Johnnie's van we passed them with their yokes. Mother asked Johnnie to stop for a minute or two. 'I want to speak to the old woman,' she told him. 'You lassies can go oot and stretch your legs.'

So we got out and I went round to the back of the cart where Bryce was. 'You are a sight for sore eyes,' he said, his own eyes aglow with pleasure. 'Why didn't you answer my letters?' he continued.

'We shifted,' I told him.

He leaned nearer and whispered 'See you tonight.'

They were going to a farm near Kirriemuir where they did the grain and potato harvest every year. As sure as his word, by seven o'clock that evening he was at the door. 'Oh, I have missed you,' he said, barely containing himself from taking me into his arms, 'I have really missed you.' Then, 'I don't suppose that you missed me very much, did you?'

'A wee, wee bit,' I answered.

'I have never gone out with any other lassie,' he went on, and wondered why I burst out laughing. 'Honest, I haven't.'

'I believe you,' I told him, laughing all the while.

51

The next two years passed with all the usual ups and downs and round-abouts.

Katie married a Brechin chap who had been asking her to be his wife for a long time. He was a non-traveller and a drover. So I got him to take out a licence for Ricky in his name. I could always say that I was looking after him for my brother-in-law. Lexy was now finished school.

Bryce and I were together whenever possible. We walked a lot around the beautiful roads at Brechin, went often to the pictures, and with that certain innocence of his he won my heart. He declared that he was delighted that I had very firmly refused to allow any sexual advances, but of course the inevitable did happen.

It was Hogmanay and we were just a wee bit high in spirit, having partaken a wee drop of the the spirit of Scotland, for the first time. How-and-ever I was little impressed by what had taken place. Far from getting any pleasure from it I had found it rather painful and disgusting, and I decided that it was not for me. Any further advances in that direction were coldly and strongly stopped. 'I cannae understand you, lassie,' Bryce would say, and I would reply, 'I cannae understand myself.' But, dear lamb that he was, he complied to my wishes. My feelings for him were still as strong.

Perhaps I should explain here how very much traveller boys and girls were kept in the dark about each other. Especially the young men. No girl or woman dare mention anything to enlighten them. Any knowledge they got was perhaps from crude jokes.

I remember meeting a young man on a bus during the war time. He was going home on leave from the Army and had had an hour or so to wait in Dundee for his connection. We talked a little then he told me that he had whiled away the time looking for a little present to take home to his mother. 'It's not easy,' I remarked, 'with everything being on coupons.'

'But I was lucky,' he told me, 'I got her towels without any coupons.'

'Never!' I exclaimed.

'Aye,' he continued, 'and they were cheap too.' Then he opened his kitbag and pulled out a brown parcel marked towels. I'm sure you can guess what kind of towels they were, and that boy was over twenty.

'Your mother will be delighted,' I said. 'Put them back in your kit-bag.' This I swear is the gospel truth. Yes, boys like that young lad, who was something of Bryce's type, were very green indeed.

However, let me get back to my story. As the weeks passed I was disturbed by the strange behaviour of my body. Oh, God, no, I thought. Surely such an unpleasant experience could not be what would make a new life? A wean, the most treasured and wonderful thing in the world? No, no, it is impossible. Quite impossible.

I soon found out that it was not impossible, but I cunningly managed to keep the fact to myself until one very cold March day. Mother and I went out to take some houses as there was no work to be had, and nothing to eat in the house. We walked out to Little Brechin and all round about there, and did manage to get a few pennies and a bag of rags.

Coming home past a little shop which used to be there, Mother went in to get half an ounce of tobacco for herself. 'Come on in wi' me,' she said. 'The woman aye keeps me cracking.' Mother's friend must have thought that I was younger, because she opened a sweetie jar and gave me a grannie sooker. I sucked the sweet while she talked, then I felt the blood leave my body and I dropped in a dwam on to the floor.

I came to in seconds in time to hear my mother ask the woman, 'What kind of sweetie was that?'

'It was just an ordinary mint sweetie. That couldnae harm her.'

Soon I felt better and when we went outside, Mother took one long look at me and sighed. 'You are the last one that I would have thocht would do this. Fine can I see now why you passed out.'

I just hung my head and didn't answer Mother, but just let her express her disappointment in me.

She lost no time in informing Bryce when he came in that night. He was astonished, as I had been, but obviously very pleased. 'We will get married as soon as possible,' he said.

'I don't want to get married,' I told him in front of Mother and Katie.

'We will have tae get married, Betsy,' he said.

'Nae "have taes" about it. I am no' gaen tae marry anybody, ever.' I was crying now.

'But the wean. . . .' He was obviously bewildered as were Katie and Mother. 'Come and I will take you to the pictures, and you might feel better.'

On our way to the cinema he said, 'Look, Betsy, if you

don't want to leave your mother, I will come and stay with you.'

'It's not that,' I told him.

'Then you don't like me enough to marry me. Is that it?'

'No!' I almost shouted the word. 'I just don't want to get married.'

We always walked along with his arm around me, uncaring about the jibes or glances of anyone. I leaned the side of my head on his shoulder and his poor heart sighed as he tightened his arm around me. 'I don't want to hurt you, Bryce. I just love to walk like this with you.'

52

All that I can remember seeing on the screen that night was Hitler, shouting and gesticulating to thousands of young Germans. Hitler youth in an almost hysterical frenzy, shouting '*Heil!*' with extended right arms. Goose-stepping soldiers, tanks, and heavy artillery filled the screen. Then Pathé News switched to Italy where Mussolini was endeavouring to outdo Hitler with his special brand of roaring.

How could all those people be so stupid, I thought. How could they allow one man to relieve them of their senses like that? I am sure that if either of those men had ordered their followers to strangle their mothers, they would have done so. Raging storms had sprung up in their brains. It was uncanny. A glisk of how very, very lacking in God's wisdom people were the world over hit me with a really hard dunt. Clattering tongues uttering driblets which soon rise up into torrents of destruction and drown the poor gullible listeners. Then I smiled at my own thoughts. Surely no-one could be more storm-tossed than myself at this moment of time?

On the way home Bryce again tried to make me change my mind about marriage. My obvious distress was most puzzling to him. However there was no way that I could bring myself to tell him nor anyone else my reason. Without any doubt

the following months were the most miserable and unhappy
of my life.

I could sleep, but food seemed to go against me. My poor
mother was out of her judgment with worry. I didn't want
to be bothered with people, only to wrestle with myself until
I was exhausted. Mother went for Jessie who came to live
with us. Even her cheery warm presence failed to raise my
spirits.

'You stay away. I don't want to see you,' I told Bryce when
no answer would come to my tired, weary mind. 'Go and find
someone else. I will never marry.'

Then he would take me in his arms and with tears in
his eyes say, 'I don't want anyone else. Only you and my
baby.'

Jessie told me that I was making everyone unhappy. This
made me feel even worse.

We did not leave the house that summer. I worked as usual
at the strawberries and rasps, but was still knotted and twisted
into a depression.

Bryce still kept coming, sometimes cycling many miles. Was
ever a poor soul so tried? He rarely brought up the subject
of marriage, but just looked at me in perplexity. I still loved
to cuddle up to him. 'I'll never understand you, Betsy,' he
would repeat. 'Never. You want me yet you don't want me.
I won't stop coming. I might even steal the wean, if you stop
me. Look, will you let your mother marry us with the Bible,
for the sake o' the wean?'

Mother had on several occasions asked me to marry Bryce
in this way. 'You will be man and wife in the eyes of God,
and you dinnae need tae worry aboot what folk say or think.'
At last I agreed and the simple ceremony was performed.

Mother sat on her knees and asked the Blessed Saviour
to be with us. 'The Blessed Saviour' were her words. 'I am
neither a minister nor a priest but I ken that you can work
through any human soul. Whether they be only a cratur like
me, or the king in a castle. This twa young folk should be
married, and by the power o' this blessed book let them be
man and wife in your sight, after they have sworn on it.'

Then Bryce and I sat on our knees, side by side with our right hands on top of the Bible, his on top of mine. 'Now,' Mother continued, 'Bryce, will you tak' Betsy for your wife and swear to be a good man to her for the rest o' your life?'

'Aye, I'll swear to that,' Bryce answered.

'Now you, Betsy. . . .' Mother looked a bit apprehensive as she held my eyes with hers. I knew that she was looking to see if I was going to be rebellious and explode or renege at the last minute.

'Ma, I cannae swear to be a good wife for the rest o' my life. I just cannae. But I could try,' I added.

'Well that's aa that's needed,' Mother said. 'A body can dae nae mair than try.'

So I swore to try to be a good wife. Mother then asked God to bless us and guide us on our travel through life.

Bryce then started to joke with me and amongst other things said, 'You are my wife now and you will do as I say.'

'I'll gie ye a wee bit o' advice, laddie,' Mother told him. 'Whatever way you may lead that one, you will never drive her. She is quiet enough gaen aboot, but the devil's ain when sair countered. I fear that she tak's after mysel' in that.'

53

Golden August introduced her even more beautiful sister September, whose gold and russet beauty was spoiled for many that year by the foolishness and ignorance of mankind. War had been declared on the very first week of her reign, and the tense, hectic bustling required to cope with it blinded many eyes to the incomparable glory of that September.

Sandbags seemed to appear by magic, built up every few yards on the outside of pavements, especially in front of big shop windows. Every peek o' light after sundown was strongly imprisoned, and dare not even peep its nose out to guide anyone blundering along in this strange unfamiliar world of blackouts.

Holes like burrows for overgrown rabbits were dug all over the place. Few gardens, greens or backyards were without one. Air-raid shelters, they called them. I, who panicked even if a dress stuck on my head when taking it off, decided that those holes were not for me. To be pitted underground like a potato was beyond thinking about. Na, na, I thought, I would rather die any other way than be smothered to death in a pit. People with pens and paper in their hands appeared on every doorway, taking a very methodical census. Almost overnight, or so it seemed, every living soul had been issued with an identity card and, a little later, ration-books.

Thousands of men, the young and not so young, in spite of the pleas of wives or parents, hastened to enlist. How uniforms were provided for them all so quickly, I still don't know.

Convoys of dark green lorries packed with khaki-clad men passed through the town. Where are they all going? I wondered. The strange thing about it all was the generally high spirits. People and especially the young were elated at having work to do, and at being needed. After years of hopeless idleness, poverty and want, I am sure that at that time many of them welcomed the excitement of war. Perhaps I should rather say, the excitement of having a few shillings in their pockets. Of being able to use the strong young muscles that God had given them, on necessary work. The pleasant feeling of well-being which often follows even after the hardest physical labour is something which no one should miss out on. It is much more fulfilling than receiving a gift of a thousand pounds.

Because of my condition I was forbidden by Mother to go out potato-picking with her and Lexy and Katie. So I wandered with Ricky.

There are so many beautiful places to walk, around the old town of Brechin. Ruddy fruit trees and bushes were rife. The earth was teeming with bounteous, wholesome sheaves of every kind of grain; well, almost every kind.

Some were standing upright in stooks, others were being carted home, many more were already stacked. Most stacks were magnificent works of art, straight as a die and solid as any house.

The ploughmen vied with others on different farms to build those stacks really well, and the results were more than pleasing to the eye. The sounds of their whistling, joking, and singing were also as pleasant to the ear. I say this even although sometimes, having noticed my shape, they shouted rather distasteful jokes in my direction. I ignored them.

'Oh, Ricky, what should I do?' I said, sitting down on a fallen tree. He wagged his tail and nuzzled my legs, happy to even hear me talk. 'If only you could speak, Ricky. I am sure you could help me.' He was looking up at me with his brown hypnotic eyes. I cuddled him impulsively, saying, 'You could never be so stupid as I am, could you, my darlin' wee jugal? You would never get your mind so ravelled.'

How long I sat trying to unravel it I cannot tell. I thought of Bryce who, I knew, would be busy harvesting. I thought of his extreme patience in putting up with my behaviour for so long. Of his gentle undemanding caresses. Of the adoration in his eyes, rivalled only by Ricky's.

Yes, I thought, I really do love him. I must hurt him no more. He would surely be called up soon and what if . . .? Here my heart gave my ribs such a dunt that I gasped. I would feel too guilty to continue to live if anything happened to him. The realisation of how selfish I had been hit me, and hit me mercilessly. My thoughts then turned to Mother, Katie and Lexy. They too were suffering agonies on my behalf. I was making them all miserable, even my dog, all because I found intimacy repulsive. Would I not bear anything to see them happy again?

So now my mind was made up. I would marry Bryce legally and as soon as possible.

The soft plod of horses' feet on the grassy old road made me come back to the world around me again. Oh Lord, is it lowsing time already? They will soon be home from the tattie field, I thought. So I jumped up and ran. Yes, jumped and ran with Ricky bounding beside me. Oh, life was good, I thought. Why should I not have to bear a little displeasure, when I had so many beautiful things to enjoy?

I was singing as I peeled potatoes when Lexy and mother came in. Katie and her husband had a wee house of their own. 'Somebody is happy today,' Mother said, with a light springing into her eyes. The stars in Lexy's eyes sparkled too.

They were so pleased to hear me singing.

Jessie had gone home a month earlier, giving me up as a hopeless case. I could not open up even to her. I always have been rather secretive about personal affairs. All my friends, relations and even Bryce will only now, if they happen to read this, find out why I had been so reluctant to marry. In fact I can't understand myself writing about it. I do so with a sort of 'Should I? shouldn't I?' feeling.

'It's good tae see you eating better,' Mother declared, 'but I fear that it's a bit late for that wee wean that you are carrying. Ach maybe no', either. There maybe was enough in you to keep it nourished.' She and my two sisters had been trying to tempt me with tit-bits which were far beyond their means. My inability to eat them had sorely vexed all three of them. Bryce too had prigged with me to eat better. I felt so very stupid, and so full of remorse.

Should I write to Bryce? I wondered. No, I would surprise him when he came down on Sunday. I bought a newspaper to while away the days. I hadn't even read anything for months.

54

The brazen, aggressiveness of Mussolini and Hitler terrified me. Poor Poland was mercilessly crushed by Hitler's mighty army. Stalin too thought that he might as well get a share of the loot.

What is happening to the world? I wondered, Or rather

to the people of the world? What did they want? All that anyone needs is the health to work to pay their way; a comfy bed; couthy friends; love; the gift of sight to fill our hearts, minds, and souls with the unlimited, unending beauty of the world around us. To see the faces of loved ones and friends; people to laugh with, as lightsome as a summer day, and to cry with when sair sorrow comes. The gift of hearing the music of nature alone, never mind the abundance of other music made by gifted men. The rapture of hearing a class of children singing *Silent Night* near Christmas time. The sound of a baby saying 'Mammie' for the first time. If one lived for a thousand years there would still be more than enough to keep everyone in the world happy and well enough fed. As it was, the shortness of life made man's present behaviour seem so silly.

'A puckle fools,' I remarked to Ricky as I threw down the paper. 'Everyone in a needless state of terrification of the other. I'm sure that Auld Clootie has been let loose amongst them.'

Bryce was restored to sanity when he found my mood and mind so changed.

'The farmer wanted me to stay and work today. Now I am glad that I refused to. He's desperate to get the harvest finished. I'll come back tomorrow and bring my things,' he said.

'There is no desperate hurry,' I told him. 'You can wait till next weekend and help to bring in the harvest, and let your mother and brothers prepare themselves for your leaving.'

So it was agreed that he would come to stay the following Saturday. We lingered long before parting that night. 'I hope you dinnae change your mind again,' were his parting words.

55

However the tiniest, most beautiful, darling little daughter was born to me in the very early hours of the following Friday.

Knowing that Mother was rather tired after being out tattie-picking, I had noiselessly borne the discomfort of labour for hours. Mother, however, even in sleep had an uncanny instinct of anything being wrong. 'I thought so,' she said, when she came through to where I was in the living room.

She dressed hurriedly, got Lexy up, telling her to try to fix a blackout, and to get a fire going in the bedroom. I had just been going to bed in the dark. 'I am going for the doctor,' Mother said.

'Oh Ma, do you have to?' I asked.

'Aye, I have to. If anything went wrong we would be in trouble. So I must fetch a doctor.'

'Let me go, Ma,' Lexy asked. 'It's a long way to the doctor's house and it's cold out. It has been snowing a bit. The roads are slushy.'

'You stay with your sister,' Mother answered as she went out the door. Lexy had a bit of bother before she got the window blacked out with blankets.

Dr Lang, may his bed be in Heaven, was a jewel of a man. All the traveller people, and many other under-privileged folk in and around Brechin, had much to thank him for. He went much further than just being a good doctor. He was also a helper and often a provider as well. All that he got in payment was a pocketful of blessings and 'thank yous' most of the time. He had got up and taken Mother home in his car.

His very presence comforted me, in spite of my fear of doctors. 'I am just in fine time,' he said, 'and I will stay with you myself.' He did not have long to stay.

If the doctor was good, the nurse who arrived next day was quite the opposite. It rankled her right away to find me sitting dressed on a chair, feeding my tiny four-pound daughter. 'What's this carry on?' she shouted. 'You get back into bed at once!' This was not said in a friendly, concerned, manner but in the manner of one sorely tried with ignorant people. She was a very pretty woman in her thirties, but rather unhappy, I judged. So I complied without answering her.

The following day I had to stay abed until she came in. I had the wean cuddled in beside me. 'Give me that child!'

she cried. 'I hope you don't keep it there at night.' Then, turning to Mother, she continued, 'You should have more sense. You told the doctor that she was married too. You are just encouraging her to go out and do the same again. The whole town knows that she is not married. Yet the doctor has her down as married.' She continued in this tone as she bathed the baby. Then when the darling wee thing complied when she held her out, she said, 'This is what you will probably be doing for the rest of your young life.'

I noticed Mother's face going pale, then becoming a fiery red. 'Well, it's just like this, my dear young woman. If my lassie does, at least she will be daen it for her ain weans, and no' for other folks' weans.' Mother took the infant from her as she spoke. 'As for her not being married. . . . Here!' she shouted to Bryce. 'Come ben here a minute, laddie. That's her man there. Through a' the world, they are man and wife. I should ken. I married them myself. So I telt the doctor no lies. Just because you have had a bad time wi' some man or other, dinnae tak' it oot on my lassie.'

Now the nurse's face vied with Mother's. You could have lit a match on it. 'Who have you been talking to?' she cried, 'Who has been telling you things about me?'

'Naebody,' Mother answered.

'I want to know, and you had better tell me.' She was really upset.

'Would you believe me if I said that it was yersel' that telt me?' Mother asked her.

'You silly, ignorant lot! First you say that you married your daughter, now you're saying that I talked about myself.'

'Aye,' Mother answered, 'and I am telling the truth baith times.'

The nurse had her coat on now and was making for the door. 'You are quite mad,' she said. 'I'll tell the doctor that I refuse to come back to you kind of people.'

'You just do that, lassie. Good day to you.'

Bryce, who had made a hasty retreat back to the living room after showing himself to the nurse, came into the room. 'What is wrong with the nurse?' he asked.

'Ach, she is a poor moich creature,' Mother answered.

Bryce had come as promised on the Saturday morning. His delight at seeing his wee daughter was indescribable. She had arrived on October the third, one month exactly after war had been declared. Mother had sat up all night nursing her in her arms, on the first night of her wee life. I knew that Mother was rather perturbed by her smallness.

The very first thing that that wean tasted was a very weak toddy, which she greedily sucked in from a teaspoon. Seeing this, Mother laughed her joy. 'She is going to be all right!' she exclaimed. 'Just look at her scoff the toddy!'

The second night Bryce sat till daybreak tenderly guarding the tiny bundle. 'You sleep,' he said, kissing me and tucking me in just as tenderly. 'I'll sit here and watch that the covers don't go over her face, or in case she be's sick or anything. You have her all day.'

That wee wean was better guarded than the crown jewels for the first week or so of her life. Bryce was a source of much surprise and even amusement to Mother. The way that he would proudly push the pram, the way that he expertly bathed his wee daughter, when I was almost in tears at the first attempt, his open-hearted simplicity.

None of those things were ever to be found in the men of our breed. Nor in many men of the travelling people. Bryce was entirely without the proud masculinity which scorned feminine ways of doing. He was not ashamed to love openly. However, I decided that I would never put him in a position where my male relations could tease and sconce him mercilessly.

The weeks passed, without me giving much thought to the world. Dr Lang spent his spare time fishing and shooting, and brought rabbits on three occasions to Mother. 'See that Betsy gets a good helping,' he said. 'She badly needs building up.' Then he would depart after expressing his pleasure at the baby's progress.

Ricky was a bit bewildered at first with all the attention diverted from him to the infant. Soon, however, he began to understand that she was very precious to me, and took over the job of guardian when she was outside in her pram. He lay under it and growled aggressively if any stranger came near.

Bryce and I were legally married, very quietly, in a minister's manse. The war was almost forgotten by me. Any fighting would surely be done in faraway, countries like France or Belgium, I thought.

56

Mother and Lexy were still potato-picking when the first horror of the war to affect us occurred. Lexy, who had gone out to get milk early one morning, returned crying hysterically. We all rushed to her. 'What's wrong? What happened?' we shouted.

'Oh, Ma, the Germans have sunk young Andy Middleton's ship! Oh Mammie, it's true!' She was now in Mother's arms. 'It happened here, Ma, in Scotland, up at the Scapa Flow. They think that a submarine did it.'

We all became almost petrified for several minutes, then Mother went out to find someone who would give her details of what had happened. She had not far to go. Groups of awe-struck men and women stood at almost every gate or shop door. All in the spell of the horror. The whole town, in fact the whole country, was now in a state of shock. This, they realised, was a glisk of what to expect in this cursed war.

In a few days we learnt that young Andy had indeed been killed. The whole town mourned for the boy who had savoured so little of life's luxuries. Mother cried openly. Her tears were for the young man's mother.

I remembered how Andy and I had teased each other on his last leave. He had laughed loudly, saying, 'Sorry, no, we don't recruit big drummers in the Navy,' referring of course to my shape.

'No,' I had answered, 'I can see that they prefer strutting peacocks to display their uniforms.'

Then after more of that kind of exchange he had remarked, 'I never thought that Bryce would leave you like that. He seemed to be so fond of you.'

My protests that the fault did not lie on Bryce, he had refused to believe.

'You know I used to think that you were man-proof,' he had continued.

'I believe that to be true myself, now,' I had answered.

'Oh, sure,' he had laughed, 'another virgin birth is imminent!'

I had swiped him with a paper which I had been carrying. Now I just couldn't believe that that cheery laughter would never again be heard.

'Well, this is the one time in my life when I am glad that I have nae laddies,' Mother remarked. 'Come on, Lexy, the lorry will be here ony minute. As I have said before, and will say again—if ye dinnae want tae droon, ye maun haud yer head abeen the water. So let us go out to the field, Lexy. You will feel better than you would moping aboot the hoose.'

Bryce too was very vexed to hear about Andy. He had met him on several occasions. He stayed at home with me that day, and when we went out shopping with the wean, people were still talking about the sinking of the *Royal Oak* One could detect fear in the voices of mothers and fathers of young sons.

When the baby was over a month old, Mother said to me, 'I think it's aboot time that your man was sleeping beside you. The poor laddie will be frozen lying on that cauld floor o' the living room.'

'It *is* getting cauld at nights now.' Bryce looked at me and put an arm around me as he spoke. 'Can I come in beside you and my wee lassie?'

Mother, I am sure, had guessed the cause of my discomfort because she turned to Bryce and said, 'I think she fears that you maybe don't know about a woman who has just had a bairn.'

He got very indignant then, and exclaimed, 'I am kinda green, but I was taught that much. I'm no' a dirty bagle.'

Travelling people believed that at least three months should elapse before a man should touch his wife after childbirth.

Strangely enough the man was held responsible. Other men would have great contempt for one whose wife gave birth in only a year's time after having a baby.

Of course the three months soon rolled past, and by then I had battered my mind with apprehensive thoughts until I was in a very dreich frame of mind and body. So much so that Don Juan himself would have had the greatest difficulty getting any response from me. Yet I managed to keep Bryce in ignorance of this.

His calling-up papers came in April. He was to join the Seaforth Highlanders at Fort George.

57

The Councils over the past years had been building houses in many towns, so there were numerous old houses which they had intended to demolish. Now they had opened them up again. Travelling people were told that they should go into those old houses, as many of them had sons or husbands in the Forces. There was also the problem of their fires, which might be seen by aeroplanes.

Now there was a tiny village called Usan about three miles from Montrose, and this is where Bryce's mother was offered a house. Two of his married sisters also got houses there. It had been a fishing village, hunkering beside the rocky coast of the North Sea. Just above it were coastguards' houses, a farm, and a few cottar houses.

Bryce and I went there to visit his folks before he left for Fort George. It was no more than a row of about twenty or so wee houses facing the sea. A village without a street, only the hard-baked earth when you stepped off your door step, then a grassy slope down to the sea. Yet I was enchanted with it. About a quarter-way down a round tower seemed to grow up from one of the houses, and about three-quarters down was a pump which supplied water for all who lived in the village.

We stayed with Bryce's mother and his two brothers for three days. I had never lived so close to the sea before and its heart-rending wailing and sobbing, when I was in bed, made sleep almost impossible. Somehow it disturbed me, like the wind did sometimes when it moaned soulfully. Even in daytime I found the sea very frightening.

There were about seven non-traveller families in the village. All the rest were travellers—Stewarts, MacKenzies, MacDonalds, Whytes, and others. The tower was full of young Irish workers, men and girls. So it was a very interesting and cheery place.

There was a most pleasant atmosphere inside the wee old houses too. The iron fire-grates were in almost as good a condition as they were when installed. They shone like new. The fisher-folk who had lived there must have cared for them very much. There was no gas or electricity.

One felt free here. Free to be natural. So when Bryce asked me to stay there with his mother while he was away I readily agreed. However, I reneged when I discovered his reason and he got a glisk of the ferocity of my temper.

We were playfully inspecting the wonders of the seashore creatures, looking for agates and jumping from rock to rock as happy as the day is long, when he put his arm around me and said, 'Now I can go away with a contented mind.'

'Why?' I asked.

'Well,' he answered, 'I can be sure that you won't be speaking to any fellows.'

That did it. I gave him a push which nearly sent him into the sea and told him to go to every pit in hell, describing my idea of each one, calling him every vile name that I could think of. Then I started to pick up the plentiful stones on the shore. 'The Germans will no' need to kill you! I'll do it now, and save them the bother. If any o' your folk try to take your part, they will get the same dose! You dirty-minded so-and-so!'

He took off up and over the rocks like a mountain goat shouting, 'What's wrong wi' ye? I never said anything wrong! What's a dae wi' ye, silly lassie?'

I couldn't get him within range although I took after him

as fast as I could. So I took my spite out on the innocent sea, throwing heavy boulders into it until I tired.

Then I ran up to the village, into the house, and picked up the bairn. She was still sleeping where I had left her on her granny's bed. I put on her outdoor things then began to gather her other bits and pieces together.

'Is there anything wrang?' one of Bryce's brothers asked.

'Ask your brother when he comes in. Ask him what's wrang, and tell him not to come back near me. Keep him here.'

He threw back his head and laughed. 'Ah! I see!' he said. 'You have been havin' a wee bit tiff, have ye?'

I glowered at him saying, 'Dinnae you start. Dinnae get funny.'

He put up his two hands in mock surrender. 'I'm not sayin' a word. Not one word.'

Few travelling people try to hide the fact that they are quarrelling. They just rant on and miscaa' each other to any other traveller they happen to talk to. The listeners only take sides at the risk of having the fury of both turned towards them.

Children, too, are not much upset by the disputes of their parents or their friends' parents. They accept them as part of life, knowing that before the day is out the ferocious lions will probably be cooing doves again.

Anyway within a very short time I was ready for the road, with the baby in my arms. Her numerous wee cousins were all around me, asking to see her once more before I left.

Bryce seemed to appear from nowhere behind me as I walked up the road. 'Come back here, lassie! There are two wild bulls coming round the corner!' he shouted. 'Do you hear me? Come back wi' my bairn!'

I ignored him, but sure enough as I rounded the corner near the farm, two snorting bulls were not many yards away from me. Of course, they were being driven by the cattleman and two helpers.

By this time Bryce had caught up with me and practically threw me over the dyke at the side of the road.

'The wean, you stupid ass!' He had lifted us both and tried

to set me on my feet on the other side of the dyke, but I slipped backwards when he let me go, and landed on my back in a heap of stinking dung. I could do nothing but lie there holding the infant above me with my two arms extended, and shout abuse at him.

He took the baby and, holding it with one hand, pulled me up with his other. It was cow-dung, and both of us were almost saturated with it. Even the bairn's white shawl didn't escape.

'You wi' the face like a cat!' I shouted. 'See what you've done! I wasnae feared o' the bulls. They wouldn't have touched us.'

'They are always a bit wild, after being cooped up in the reed all winter,' he answered. 'I couldnae risk letting my two bonnie wee lassies get hurt.' He looked so silly with his feet and trouser legs, also his hands and arms, covered with cow's shern that I laughed in spite of myself.

The laughs of practically everybody in the village awaited us when we returned to get cleaned up. Bryce's oldest sister said, 'Give me the wean. I have plenty clean baby clothes. I will bath her and dress her for you.'

Her two oldest girls ran and filled two blackened buckets with water. Bryce's mother hung one on the swey above the fire and his sister put the other one on her fire. The girls brought more water in their clean pails and emptied them into a large zinc bath. This was all accompanied by much giggling. Soon we had a bath half full of nice warm water, which was carried into a tiny bedroom. 'Put the sneck on the door and then the wee yins winnae get in,' Jeanie, Bryce's sister, said.

As Bryce scrubbed the muck off my back he said, 'I didnae mean any harm by what I said to you.'

'Don't remind me,' I told him. 'You couldn't have been more insulting. You as good as said that I needed to be guarded by your folks to keep me from going with men.'

'No, no, I didnae mean that at a'. As sure as God I didnae mean that.'

'Yes, you did. You said it, and you meant it.' I was quite calm now. 'Look, Bryce,' I went on, 'I am not going to be a victim of your jealous nature. You have a problem there, and if you're not careful it will do you harm.'

Bryce had no difficulty in getting clean clothes to put on from his brothers. I too was given one of his niece's best clothes. She insisted, eager to please. My heart went out to those dear people.

The only trouble was that I had bigger feet than any of the women or girls. Bryce's mother was vexed and said, 'Look at that bonnie shoe. It's just your size, but I burned the marrow o' it.'

'Here is another one my size,' I exclaimed, rummaging among a bag of old shoes.

'Might ye care, lassie. I'm sure that it has no neighbour either.'

Luckily the two shoes were for opposite feet, so I put them on.

'You cannae gang hame wi' two marrowless shoes,' Bryce said. 'Everybody will laugh at you. I'm no' walking about wi' ye like that.'

'Well if everybody gets a laugh at me, it will maybe dae their hearts good, and if you dinnae want tae be seen wi' me, you can bide. I cannae put on my own shoes, the cow's shern has soaked right through them.' So I went home in marrowless shoes.

'You are an affie lassie, Betsy,' his sister Jeannie said on parting. 'I couldnae hae the neck tae dae that.'

58

Mother and Lexy had been out potato-planting. Neither of them showed much surprise at my footwear. 'You are well shod the day,' Mother ventured. 'That was surely a good smith that ye went tae.'

'Aye,' I laughingly answered, then explained to them what had happened.

Lexy had a pot of porridge ploop-plooping away on the

gas ring, and was making pancakes on the fire, stopping now and then to rub her eyelids. 'You finish making the pancakes, Betsy. 'I've got wildsleeps. Somebody must be coming this very night.'

'Ach, maybe it's out-sleeps that you have,' I answered.

'I've had sleeps aa' day as well,' Mother told us. 'I'm sure somebody else is coming too. In-sleeps I have. The same as Lexy.'

All travelling people talk of having sleeps. If they are bothered with itchy eyelids all day, they call it in-sleeps, which means that someone is coming to stay the night. If it is their eyebrows that itch, then it is called out-sleeps, meaning that someone who lives in the house won't be sleeping in it that night. They get a bit upset and anxious if they get out-sleeps, lest anything happens to one of the household.

Sure enough, when Lexy answered a knock at the door, who should be standing there but a young soldier called Willie Kerr. He was one of the boys who had been brought up beside us, one of the gang I mentioned before. He looked wonderful. He was a regular soldier, having joined the Boys' Service when very young. He had his kit with him.

We all welcomed him and admired his changed physique. 'Laddie, the Army agrees wi' you,' Mother told him.

'I wondered if you had any idea where my father is,' he said. 'I'm on embarkation leave. I've been to see my two sisters. Nora is married now, and Hattie is working in a hotel in Aberdeen, but neither of them knows where he is.' Willie's father had taken to going from town to town, staying in lodging houses, since the loss of his wife and the family leaving home.

'Oh, now,' Bryce told him, 'you havenae far tae go.'

'That's right,' I added. 'We were speaking to him today. He's in Usan.'

'Usan?' Willie echoed. 'Where in the name o' God is that? I've never heard o' it.'

'No,' Bryce answered. 'It's just a wee, wee placie near Montrose. He is biding wi' his cousin's wife there. He goes to Montrose and round about playing his melodeon.'

Willie took Mother and Lexy to the pictures so Bryce and I sat playing with our wee daughter and talking. He sang lullabies to her and his tender expression as he gazed on her wee face really touched my heart. He sang so beautifully too.

'I'm going to miss you two terribly,' he said, tears glistening in his eyes. 'My wee lassie is thriving like a bracken.' Wee Mary was very like her dad, with black hair, long for a wean's, and blue eyes. But Bryce has hazel eyes.

'Curse Hitler! Curse Mussolini! And Stalin, and all the mad-men that make bloody wars!' he burst out.

I sat down on the sofa beside him. 'I feel just the same,' I told him. 'Oh, Bryce, I just dinnae want to think about it.' Then in a desperation of pity, love, and sympathy I became tremulous and the tears came.

Bryce rose up and put the wean in its pram, then put out the light and returned to me. His first kiss released floods of emotions which had been under lock and key somewhere inside of me. Now they welled up and completely overpowered me in indescribable ecstasy. Don't wake me from this dream, I thought. Don't ever wake me up.

Next day Willie Kerr left to look for his father. 'If I were you I would get a taxi in Montrose to take you to Usan,' Bryce told him. 'It is a bit far to carry your kit and rifle and everything.'

He thanked us then bade us farewell. 'See you on my next leave,' he said. 'I will drop by.'

However we were never to see him again. Not all that long after that, I heard that he too was a victim of the monstrous war.

Mother and Lexy were out at work, while Bryce and I were in an enchanted little world all day. In Mother's words, a time of rowans and wild honey: the rowans being the bitterness of having to part the next day, the honey being the delicious sweetness of our last day together before parting.

'Life is a mixture o' rowans and wild honey. We maun hae the bitter tae mak' us appreciate the sweet!' Mother used this expression to any folk feeling sorry for themselves.

59

No more than a week after Bryce went away, Mother and Lexy went to see our oldest sister Bella, and returned to tell us that she had gotten a house up in Coupar Angus. 'I have never really been settled here since your father died,' she said. 'So I will be happier and less lonely nearer Bella and the rest of them in Blairgowrie.' Lexy and I were pleased and excited about this. We too felt a bit far away from our ain folk.

As nearly all our young cousins had joined up, we had no one to come and take us up there. Mother just got a man who dealt in second-hand furniture to come and clear out the house, after letting Katie take anything that she wanted.

We arrived in Coupar Angus with only a few blankets, dishes, and Mother's kist which held her few treasures. The house did not have the facilities of our Council one in Brechin. No bathroom nor inside toilet, but it was cosy and we soon picked up bits and pieces of furniture for it. It was heavenly being able to walk the five miles to Blairgowrie to see Jessie and all the other relations who lived there. Or having them visit us.

Bryce wrote at least three times every week, so the time passed quickly. Since the sinking of the *Royal Oak* I had been buying papers and keeping up with what was happening in the war.

As the months passed our hectic preparations for invasion and air-raids seemed to have been needless. Propaganda was rife and so the bulk of British people were smug and felt safe—confident that our troops in France, and the Royal Navy, would soon put Germany in her place. The power of words when spoken by Churchill had filled the hearts of the people with confidence and determination and the will to face bravely, if needs be, the formidable enemies.

But in the summer of 1940 our laddies who had rushed to join up so cheerfully and optimistically, singing *Hang up*

your Washing on the Siegfried Line or *Run, Rabbit Run,*
were doing the running, fleeing for dear life towards the
Channel. Many did not make it, but were taken prisoner
or killed on the way. Many more died before they could
get transport across the Channel, and many others on the
beaches or during the crossing.

Aunt Nancy, who had three sons in France, was grateful to
have Mother's support during that trying time. Had Mother
foreseen this, I wondered. Was this the main reason for her
coming to be near her sister?

However, Aunt Nancy's sons did escape at different times
but she and Uncle Andy had aged visibly during the ordeal
of waiting for news of the boys.

60

At that time I received a letter from Bryce saying that he
had been transferred to Aberdeen, attached to the Gordon
Highlanders. 'Will you please come through?' he wrote. 'My
sister Phemie has a house in Aberdeen, and will be pleased
to have you live with her.'

Mother was a bit vexed at my leaving, but said, 'You go
to where your man is. It is only right that you should be
beside him. Lexy and I will be all right here. Take care o'
the wean.'

I had never been far away from Mother and Aberdeen
seemed as remote as China does now. However I was young
and eager to be with Bryce again.

There were several traveller boys just back from Dunkirk
in the carriage of the train in which I went to Aberdeen. I
didn't know any of them but after listening to them talking
in the cant, I thought that I had better let them know that
I too was a traveller. Especially when they began to discuss
me jocularly! Soon they were all around me, holding wee
Mary, plying her with chocolate and pennies. I'm sure I
must have asked them a hundred questions. They appeared

dazed, bewildered, and so very, very glad to be in Scotland again.

Bryce's sister's husband, who had only one leg, met me at the station. He turned out to be a jolly, devil-me-care fellow and very cheery, pleasant company. He had, however, the restless spirit which often accompanied his illness, tuberculosis of the bone. Bryce's sister was very much like Bryce, not only in appearance but also in nature. We got on fine and now and then Bryce managed to get down to the house.

At this very precarious time, invasion was imminent so soldiers had to be on the spot, as it were, and were not allowed away from their regiment very much. He had pleaded for permission to stay even for one night at his sister's house with me, but had been firmly refused. I thought this funny. Although the country was in peril, I just couldn't see my gentle, rather timid, husband doing much about it. That of course was the thinking of a rather stupid young mind.

On more than one occasion I was told, 'Get to hell out of here!' by the guards as I waited to try and get a few minutes with him. Did I know then that prostitutes often hung around the gates of barracks, just as I was doing? I'm afraid I was still like Bryce—rather green. Bryce's sister always offered to keep wee Mary, who was a little gem, so I did not have her with me on those occasions.

Some nights he did get a pass-out until twelve o'clock. I remember one such night when we were sitting in a picture house. The siren sounded, and its dreary groaning wail was the signal for Bryce to return to his barracks immediately. The tramcars had to stop when the siren went off and we were about three miles from his sister's house.

'There is folk going to an air-raid shelter,' Bryce told me. 'You go with them until the all-clear sounds.'

'Oh no,' I answered. 'No air-raid shelter for me. I will just walk home.'

'Trust you to be thrawn. Ye ken I've got to go back to the barracks.' Bryce was annoyed now.

'I'm not stopping you from going back, but if the devil himself was chasing me I wouldn't go into one o' those holes in the ground. Not even if the Pope o' Rome asked me.'

I could almost feel Bryce struggle with himself. He was rather timid in the face of authority, and his fear of authority overcame his concern for me. 'I must go,' he said. 'Do you know your way back to the house?'

'I will find it,' I said. 'You run. Go on, run.'

'Will you bring the wean down to the park tomorrow? We will be doing drill down there,' he asked quite unsuspectingly.

'Like hell I will. I'll be many miles away, baith me and the wean. You run, like a good wee laddie. You would just dae the same if Hitler's bombs were comin' doon in showers. Nae wonder I was warned aboot a laich dyke. Much laicher ye couldnae get.'

I was away over Bryce's head now. 'What are ye speakin' aboot dykes for? What's wrong wi' ye, lassie? You just could-nae be like onybody else could ye, and go tae the shelter?'

'Aye, and walk three miles hame in the black-oot, but don't worry. I am going to be like Felix and keep on walking as soon as daylight comes. You stay here and jump half a mile in the air every time duty calls.'

There were still a few people on the street. So I walked away from him and shouted to a man, 'Hey, mannie, could ye tell me how to get tae the Bridge o' Don?'

'Nae bother, my lass. In fact I'll easy tak' ye there if ye like.'

He was a good-natured man and when Bryce came up and said, 'This is my wife and I think I'll tak' her hame mysel',' the man replied, 'Well I would if I were you.'

'See,' I said.

'Aye, I see noo,' Bryce answered. 'I just wasnae thinkin' richt.'

'If that's gaen tae be your way o' thinkin' then ye can leave me oot o' yer thinkin',' I answered. 'I cannae help it if I get intae trouble.'

Who was really thinking right I still don't know. Anyway, we were back on warm cuddly terms by the time we got to his worried sister's house.

When I went to the Duffy Park the next day with the

bairn, he came over during a break in drill and was all smiles.

'I didnae get intae bother,' he told me.

'I didnae think you would,' I answered.

61

Bryce's sister Phemie had four children. The oldest, a boy of ten, was away with his paternal grandparents in the country, camping. Travelling people nearly always allowed a child to go with their elderly parents. The boy would be a help to them, and company.

The old folk had a house next door to Phemie, but in spite of having three married sons away in the Forces, they just couldn't content themselves in the house all summer. However, old Donald the husband came in from the country once every week to see if there were any letters for him. He could not read himself but got Phemie to read them for him.

There was a letter for him the first time that I saw him. Two of his sons had come safely home, but a much loved grandson had been killed. So he was anxious to have the letter read.

His first words were 'Any word o' Duncan yet?'

Phemie's husband, who was Duncan's twin, just shook his head, saying, 'No, Father, not yet.'

'I doot, I doot,' the auld man continued, 'aye, I doot he's no' comin' back. Aa the laddies are hame noo.'

'Ach, he could be a prisoner, Dad. Dinnae think like that.'

Phemie, who had been silently reading the letter, handed it to her husband. Her face had paled. Hughie her husband read it, then said, 'This letter's from Sandy, Dad. He says that he was on a ship with Duncan and that it got a direct hit. He is in London, but he has not seen nor heard anything of Duncan since the ship went down.'

'Oh my God. . . .' the old man began.

'Dinnae, Dad,' Hughie said. 'Duncan must be all right. I would ken, Dad, if he wasnae. I have never had any feeling that Duncan was gone. He will be dropping in any day now. I'm sure he will, Dad.' Hughie's words did much to calm his father.

'I'm gaen awa' doon tae see Duncan's wife,' he said. 'You, lassie, put on your coat and come doon wi' us.' These were his first words to me. 'You are young Bryce's wife, aren't you? A real Perthshire ranny. What dae ye think o' the bread and milk country?'

'I havenae seen much o' it yet,' I answered.

'Well, get the coat on. I want Jean my wife tae see ye. She is fae your side o' the country.'

I did as he asked, and followed him out with Mary in my arms. Hughie too came with us.

Jessie, Duncan's wife, was down on her knees washing the floor when we got there. We heard her singing as we came up the stairs. 'Aye you're happy, quean,' old Donald greeted her.

'Well, auld yin, it doesnae make onything better gaen aboot wi' a sour face.' She rose up saying, 'Come awa' in and sit doon and get a mouthful o' tea.'

'You'll maybe no' be so happy at what I've got tae tell ye,' auld Donald went on.

'What noo are ye come tae tell me?' I noticed that Jessie was big with child.

'Far be it fae me tae spoil your happiness, but it's quite possible that your man is lying at the bottom o' the Channel.' He handed her the letter as he spoke.

She read it then shook her head saying, 'Na, na, there never was the German born that could kill Duncan. Anyway I would ken. I'm sure I would ken.'

'That's what I say tae,' Hughie put in. 'He's my identical twin and I always seem tae ken if Duncan is in dire straits.'

'I've got a drappie whisky here, will I put it in your tea?' Jessie asked old Donald.

'Na, I'll tak' it as it is,' he answered. Jessie then gave Hughie and me tea.

'How do you like Aberdeen?' she asked me. Then, 'You must be Bryce's wife.'

'Aberdeen is beautiful,' I answered, 'I have never stayed in a big city before. There is so much to see.'

'Have you told auld Jean about this letter?' Jessie asked Donald.

'Na, and I'm no' gaun tae tell her. If you twa are sae sure that Duncan's all right, then there's nae sense worrying her needlessly. I'm just gaun away tae meet her noo. She went awa' tae buy a wee pickle stock, tae sell in the country. Are ye comin', lassie?' he finished, turning to me.

'What are ye needin' the quean wi' ye for?' Jessie asked.

'Well, it's just like this. I cannae gang awa' oot tae the country again withoot kennin' aboot Duncan and if I just said tae Jean we'll bide in the hoose for a day or twa', she would ken that I was worried. On the other hand if she gets this lassie tae question aboot a' her breed and generation, she just might ask to bide hersel'. Ye ken what like she is when she meets somebody fae the highlands o' Perthshire.

'You're a fly auld hairy,' Jessie told him. Then she turned to me, saying, 'She is an auld tartar, but never heed her.'

Auld Jean was a very striking woman with dark hair, dark eyes and complexion. She wore long gold earrings, a black sateen apron, and fisher-girls' petticoats. She was in fact a real traveller. The eyes missed nothing as they took me in.

Then she scanned the bairn. 'Did you ca' her Mary?' she asked. When I nodded, she went on, 'You couldna ca' her anything else, could you? She is Brycie's mother's spit.'

'That's exactly what my mother said,' I told her.

'So Duncan's no' hame yet?' she said addressing Donald.

'No, but there's hundreds as weel as him. He'll drop in any day noo.'

A letter did arrive from Duncan a couple of days after that. Long days indeed for the anxious old couple. The old man tramped around the houses of his friends and married family. The old woman passed her time by putting me through a sort of third degree. I humoured her even when she sought to enlighten me on the worthlessness and stupidity of some

161

of my forbears. 'Fine I mind on your grandfather's brother Jeck.' Then she would change her note, suddenly saying, 'For a' that, many a time I was gled tae see him. He used tae empty his pockets and scatter pennies tae a' the weans. He was a grand piper and could get money quicker than some folk could get slate stanes.'

When Donald brought home the news that Duncan was home there was a lilt in the air. 'He is too tired to come down to see you tonight,' he told her.

62

The following evening Duncan came to see his parents. He was a chip off the old block. Even an empty house would have come to life with his presence. Phemie's weans were all over him. He had us all in high spirits within minutes. One immediately felt at ease with him.

They decided to have a little celebration in Phemie's house and I was sent out for drink. They tended to treat me as a child, although I was nineteen.

'Duncan, tell us aboot the fighting in France,' old Donald asked, after a while.

'Fighting?' Duncan echoed. 'I never was in any fighting. Sandy and me were stationed at a place ca'd Rouen, attached tae a medical corps. We were guarding the station with bren guns. I never even saw a German. The only Germans were in planes—but there were plenty o' them, bombing and machine-gunning. For three nights and three days we got no sleep. We didn't want to leave the wounded.

'Anyway, we got orders to get ready to leave, so we started to walk, or march I should say. We had a very young lieutenant, but a good one. We marched for days and other troops and men who had lost their regiments were joining the ranks. Maist o' the lads were in agony wi' blistered feet, but Sandy and me had nae bother that way. We were so used to walking.

'We stopped for a break, I couldnae tell ye whar. Onywye, Sandy and me slipped awa' tae a toon nearby. We were starving wi' hunger. When we got tae the toon we asked a man for food and drink. "Come, come," he said, "this way." We followed him and he took keys oot o' his pocket and opened a door. It was a quarter-master's store. There was cases and cases o' Dewar's whisky, beers, rum, and tons o' food. The man just gestured to it and said, "British all gone, leave everything."

'Well, I couped everything oot o' my kit bag. So did Sandy.

'Then we packed them wi' corned beef and anything that we thought we could carry. I took three bottles o' the whisky as well. At the same time I would have swapped a gallon o' whisky for one sip o' tea. We shared wi' the lads nearest us, but I kept one o' the bottles o' whisky in my kit bag, meaning tae tak' it hame.

'I cannae tell ye how many times we had tae dive intae ditches or flatten ourselves on the ground. Then we just had tae march on and leave the dead and wounded.

'One day a convoy o' fourteen trucks came along. Our young lieutenant stopped them. They were all empty at the back. The lieutenant in charge refused to allow us to board the trucks. I watched the two commanders argue about that, then our young officer drew his revolver and, as I had sidled closer, I heard him say, "I will use this if necessary. My men are footsore and exhausted, and you want to drive past with fourteen empty trucks. I am taking them over, and any more protests from you will make me leave you here, to walk." That's the kind o' fellow he was, our lieutenant. He did his own thinkin'.

'"My orders were not to stop till I reached the Channel shore," the other officer stated.

'"Don't worry about that. I am giving the orders now, and I will take full responsibility for them." Our lieutenant was gesticulating to us to board the trucks as he spoke. Anyway we were all thankful to him for getting us off our feet. Most o' us fell asleep in the trucks.

'When we finally stopped we were at a place called Saint Nazaire. The beach was thrang wi' men dodging machine-gun bullets. I heard big gunfire, and noticed that it was coming from a ship, a British ship. Our officer beckoned us towards it after he had driven a few more miles.

'The ship was called the *Lancastria* and somehow he got us all aboard without panic, in spite of the chaos and thundering noise all around us. There must have been thousands of men aboard the *Lancastria*. Sandy and me stuck close together all the time, and our first race was to the bar. A destroyer called the *Havelock* accompanied the *Lancastria*, and maybe it was its guns that I had heard.

'After drinking a pint, which tasted better than a mother's milk to a wean, I told Sandy that I was going to the toilet. I wasnae minutes in the toilets when a noise like the thunders o' hell nearly burst my ears. The ship shuddered violently and I was hurled reel-rall against the waa'.

'There were two other fellows in the toilets, a big English chap and a fellow Scot. We pulled open the door, but the stairway had gone. Luckily there were three portholes in the toilets. Two o' them were stuck with rust, but we did get one open after a struggle. "You go first," I told the English fellow. I nearly regretted my words. His big behind stuck in the porthole and this young laddie and me pushed and pushed without budging him an inch. In the end I got my boot against his backside and with the other boy half holding me up and pushing as well, I came three hard dunts off him wi' my heavy boots. That did the trick.

' "Bloody hell, Jock," I heard him shout. He waited and pulled me and the other chap through the portholes though. "This ship's going down, mate. Get to hell off it as soon as you can."

' "I cannae swim," I told him, "so it's six and half-a-dozen what I dae."

'The noise of shouting, screaming, tramping, and splintering wood was all around me. The two lads had disappeared amangst the scuddlin' thrang. It's a pity that I didnae hae the bottle o' whisky, I thought. I could have drunk the lot and never felt a thing.

'Just then wha should tap me on the shoulder but the big Englishman. "Here you are, Jock. Get into this," he said, helping me into a life-jacket. "Now listen, Jock. Keep your chin well up when you hit the water. These bloody things could break your bloody neck. Then paddle like hell away from the ship." He seemed tae ken what he was talkin' about, so I just did as he said.

'Jerry was still sending the machine-gun bullets down. The water was dotted wi' poor souls. I kept paddling wi' my hands, like the chap told me.

'Then I thought that I heard voices singing. I turned around and it was not my imagination. The singing was coming from the Lancastria, and she was sinking. The strains of *There'll always be an England* gave my heart such a dunt that I grat like a bairn. I watched the *Lancastria* go down, but the sight and sound will be with me till God calls on me. You've got to hand it to they English. I tell you, nothing that ever happens to me in the future could affect me more. Not if I live to be a hundred.

'Anyway, I was picked up by a French tug. They gave me a curtain to wrap around me when I took off my wet clothes. Then with nothing but the curtain around me I was transferred to another ship, the *Oronsay*. I landed at Plymouth. The Red Cross lassies were waiting with cups o' tea and sandwiches. I was never so glad to get a cup o' tea in my life.

'I had to go to Plymouth railway station, still in the curtain. If I could have taken a train hame tae Aberdeen I would have done it. However I had nae claes, nae money, nae nothing. So I had to report to the headquarters in Plymouth where they found a uniform for me and arranged for me to go to London, to Wembley Stadium. It was packed wi' soldiers, not all British.

'Then I was a few days in the Crystal Palace before being sent out to Dartmoor. I never saw nor heard o' what happened tae our lieutenant. His name was Sim and I think he came from Lossiemouth.

'Dartmoor was a mass o' tents, and the very next day after

I was sent there the officer in charge asked a corporal to fetch me. What can he be wantin' me for? I wondered.

'When I went to the officer's tent who was standing there but the bold boy Sandy. Well, did ever you see two grown men huggin' and kissing one another like lassies. We had both thought that the other had gone down with the *Lancastria*. Sandy had been picked up by the *Havelock*.

'When we could get the breath tae speak, Sandy said, "God, cove, I have written to your father and mother saying that I thought you had gone down with the ship." That's why I wrote to you myself. I was so dazed and confused before that. I didnae really ken what I was daein.

'We asked the officer for leave to go home and he gave us the papers and four pounds ten shillings each. So here I am, back in God's country, auld Scotland.'

We had all sat listening spellbound to Duncan's story. Even the bairns never uttered a word. Old Donald broke the spell by saying, 'Aye, it's a bitty different noo tae what it was like when I was in France.'

63

I stayed in Aberdeen until Bryce asked me to leave. It was after one night when quite a few bombs had fallen on the city. The Bridge of Don barracks had been hit. It was only a few blocks away from us and Phemie's house got such a shake that the furniture seemed to be dancing about in it. I was rather frightened and, lifting wee Mary in my arms, would have run outside. 'Don't go out,' Phemie said. 'Listen, that's machine-gun fire.' So we sat in the lobby with our backs against the wall. There had been no warning siren.

As I listened to the blasts of bombs, I prayed that they would not hurt Bryce. Phemie too was anxious about her restless, roving husband. He could be in any part of the city. When he did come home much later he immediately put my mind at rest about Bryce. 'I happened to be near Summer Street,' he told me. 'Nothing dropped near there.'

It was the following day that Bryce told me to go away out of Aberdeen. 'We are all going,' Hughie told him. So we went to Usan, to stay with Bryce's mother. I would much rather have gone home to my own mother, but I wanted to please Bryce and give him as little worry as possible.

I found life in Usan very pleasant. Bryce's people could not have been nicer, but I missed the charm of my own wayward unpredictable folks. I especially missed Mother, and her ready laughter.

Mother always judged people by their sense of humour. On meeting anyone for the first time, she often would utter some witticism or other to see how they would react. If she found them lacking in sense of humour she had little regard for their type of intelligence. Sense and a sense of humour went hand-in-hand according to Mother's way of thinking.

I felt a wistful longing to be with her again. So I just got ready and went. Bryce's Mother was a bit upset at my leaving. 'He will no' be very pleased wi' ye,' she said, meaning Bryce. 'He may even think that we havenae been good tae ye.'

'I just want to be with my ain folk, Granny.' Everyone of the family called her Granny. 'You have been more than good to me. Bryce will just have to understand.'

64

I went home by train, but found the house empty when I got there. It was potato-picking time again, early potatoes. I soon gained access through a window, then tidied up and prepared a nice meal for them coming home.

Lexy's loud 'Ah-h!' as she ran to hug me was very heart-warming. 'Ma, you were right. How did you ken that it was Betsy's sleeps that we have had all day?'

Mother, washing her hands, replied, 'I am never far wrang.'

She immediately picked up wee Mary who was now propelling herself about in a most peculiar manner. She stuck out one leg then pulled the rest of her up to it.

'It's fine to come hame tae a big fire and a warm tasty feed,' Mother said after a while. 'I think I'll hire you. How much do you charge a week?'

'Two or three puffs o' your auld cutty-pipe,' I answered. 'I have been smoking nothing but fags since I went awa'.'

'Well I think we could just about manage that,' she laughingly replied.

Katie's husband was called up soon after that and she came to join us. She also had a wee daughter now, so we took day about looking after the weans and working at a farm about two miles out the road. We did all types of farm work, because of the scarcity of men. The farmer never insisted that we started and finished with his regular workers. He just told us what he wanted done and let us get on with it in our own way.

Ricky was never more than inches away from me, and almost wept every time I went out without him, lest I should be going away again. This in spite of the fact that the others were more than good to him. There seemed to be an invisible connection between his little warm heart and mine.

I took him with me when working, and took him and Mary for long walks when not. Sometimes to where the Isla water sang softly, old melancholy airs. Sometimes to where a wee bickerin' burn noisily scolded every stone that it louped over. Sometimes through old overgrown byways, where we ate the abundant winter fruit—haws, brambles and rose-hips. Ricky seemed to enjoy them as much as I did, after I had de-seeded them for him.

He even seemed to share my delight in exploring any old ruin that we should come across. If the old wall-stones had an atmosphere of peace, happiness and tranquillity, we would linger there—me trying to make a picture in my mind of the cottage and its occupants in days gone by. However, if within the old wall-stones there was a sinister eerie atmosphere, he was the first to dash out and refuse to enter again. He would even meek a little as if saying, 'Come away from there,' and when I did he would bound around me, tail wagging rapidly.

Sometimes he would sniff out rabbits in the undergrowth, and even catch a young one and carry it ever so gently back to me, then look up into my face for instructions. 'No, Ricky,' was all that I needed to say to make him release it. Then we would watch it scamper away quite unharmed, but very scared. Sometimes wee Mary would sit up and take an interest, chuckling her delight at the antics of Ricky and her crazy Mum. Mostly she preferred to sleep and let us be to behave as we were wont.

On the way home I daydreamed. Ricky, I am almost sure, did the same as he just trotted quietly along at my heel. My dreams were never very ambitious. I dreamt of Bryce with a pleasant warmth. Would I be able to give him and my children happiness? What future would there be for us if Hitler's crazy puppets should invade, and conquer these pleasant islands? Already they were mercilessly slaughtering every gypsy that they came across. Not to mention the Jews, and they would certainly class us as types of gypsies.

I conjured up many ideas in my mind, from escape to neutral Ireland to pretending to be non-travellers. Even to what would be the easiest and least painful way of relieving Hitler's madmen of the task of annihilating us. Then I would switch my dreams to a more pleasant sphere. I would be the mistress of a little croft with a few acres of land. Bryce and I would keep a cow for milk, a horse to help us till the soil. Some hens, ducks and geese. Ricky, and some pussy cats. We would have our friends and relations there with their musical instruments, their diddling, canterach and singing. We could enjoy the high-spirited philosophy of the travelling people, whilst treating them to our home-grown, home-made goodies.

Ah sweet, sweet dreams. Inevitably my dreams leaned towards Mother. Where could I find her marrow? Where was there anyone with her almost uncanny insight, her unnerving capacity to judge, her quick diagnosis of what ailed people?

Dreams of Mother usually gave my heart a dunt which sent the dreams scooring, and made me hasten my steps. She and the girls would be coming home to an empty house with no bright fire or warm supper. Time I could not tether, so why did I waste it, I thought.

65

Brechin almost groaned with the weight of evacuees from big cities, Polish soldiers and all manner of refugees from bombed homes. Even the woods around were hotching with soldiers, all training and preparing for invasion. The shops were already bare of everything that hinted of luxury and little treats were hard to find. Yet as I passed a makeshift quarter-master's store, where soldiers were unloading, my eyes bulged nearly out of my head at the sight of so much of the fruits and other delights that had disappeared from the shops.

I stopped and stood a bit away, gaping. It was on a quiet back street. Suddenly the young truck-driver sped towards me carrying something, then with a quick flip of the pram-cover had secreted it in the pram beside wee Mary. I hurried away then had a peek under Mary's cover. A very long tin of corned beef, a pound or more of coffee beans, a few oranges and dried fruit. Oh Lord, I thought, may you always answer my unsaid prayers so speedily. Then I ran towards the house with Ricky at my heels. Champed tatties, neeps and stacks of lean corned beef. Then oodles of coffee and sweet dates. Oranges for the weans. A feed fit for the King, I thought.

Bryce came home on leave shortly after than and pleaded with me to come back to Aberdeen. 'We are to be leaving Aberdeen soon,' he said. 'Anyway, there are no air-raids there now.'

'You should be where your man is,' Mother told me.

So we went back to spend the rest of his leave in Usan, then to Aberdeen, where I stayed until February when Bryce was sent down to England. There was much bombing of the big cities in England. Bryce was in Liverpool and Birmingham. Both of those places were more dangerous than the actual front. He had been transferred to the Pioneer Corps.

We went out to live at the farms in spring and summer. Other travellers were there as well, so in spite of the war we had lovely times.

I was with child again but this was the expected and accepted thing. Traveller women made no fuss about having babies, but if any traveller men were around, the expectant mother had to conceal her condition as much as possible. Men got very embarrassed if openly spoken to by a woman 'wi' her belly tae her moo' as they put it. Shameless hussies, they described them. Older women thought this way too. They had always worn shawls when pregnant. So I had to be very careful when we went to work at the turnip-thinning on a farm in the Carse o' Gowrie. A family called Reid and a family of McDonalds were also there. Altogether there were five men, three quite young. With my first child there had been no problem with this as there had been few travellers living in Brechin. Now, however, I had to wear a sort of box-jacket even on warm days.

In spite of rationing the old woman Reid often brought a wee treat to me when she returned from shopping. A banana, perhaps, or an orange. Such things were almost impossible to find in any shop at that time, but auld Clemmie Reid was an uncannily gifted spey-wife and shop-owners would gladly give her them, if they had them, in return for having their palm read. Piper Davie, her husband, also pampered me by bringing back a bottle of milk stout when he went for a pint.

The McDonalds too, were the hearts of corn, taking my mother to the shops in their yokes and bringing all the firewood that we needed. It was difficult to believe the horrors that were going on throughout the world, as we worked at our leisure in the middle of the quiet lovely countryside.

We travelled with those families that summer to several

different farms. Sometimes the farms were quite a bit apart, and at our walking pace we couldn't make it in one day. The elderly and the weans, and all our bits and pieces, were big enough loads for the two ponies.

On two of these occasions we had some bother finding a place to stay. The old camping sites which we had intended staying on were fenced off and had notice-boards put up threatening prosecution to anyone disregarding the signs.

At that time travelling people feared to offend authority. We were rather footsore and weary by the time that we came across somewhere to unharness the tired ponies and flop down with a blanket on the ground, afraid to make a fire to boil water for a cup of tea.

Old Piper Davie cursed the powers that be. 'What's the world comin' tae? Could the Germans be ony worse than the silly bastards here?' he ranted. I could have told him just how much worse, but didn't. I would have made him an enemy for sure. 'What's my three laddies and my twa godsons fighting for? Could onybody tell me that?' he went on, speaking to no one in particular. 'It would be well done if the Germans did come and troosh and snool them and chase them fae pillar tae post, the way that they dae tae us. Worse than swine they mak' us. Aye, twenty thousand times worse!'

'Wheesht ony mair the nicht,' auld Clemmie chided him. 'Ganching will no mak' things ony better. If you had the pain o' my twa heels you would hae something tae ganch aboot. They are skinned tae the bone.'

'Well, it's yer ain faet. Ye had nae need tae travel. I telt ye tae come intae the cairt.'

'Would you twa auld folk baith wheesht, and let the weans get a wee sleep?' This from one of their daughters-in-law.

Auld Davie was determined to have the last word and as he tried to make himself comfortable on the hard earth he muttered, 'Nae wonner. Nae bloody wonner when a body has tae dae this!'

66

At the end of September we all reluctantly went back to our houses. It was getting near my time.

Part of Meikleour Castle had been given over for a maternity hospital. The wooded grounds too were at the disposal of the Army. Come November and I landed in there. I had no option. The doctors all around sent their patients there to have their babies.

It was a rather isolated place and difficult to get transport to, but Mother and the girls walked to see me. I had hung on until I knew that the baby would not be long in entering the world. I was the only patient with a baby so I was in a room by myself. A little middle-aged nurse came in and put out the lights after ensuring that I was all right.

My attempts to sleep were spoiled by a rustling sound which went from one end of the room to the other. Leaves, I thought, blowing in through the window. So up I got and went to the window only to find it closed. I was upstairs, and looking out I saw two deer searching for food. It was a cold night with the white rime glistening on the trees and grounds. I could see how beautiful the surroundings of the castle were in the light of the full moon. I could not see any leaves or anything that could possibly be making the rustle. Anyway there was no wind.

I was on my way back to bed when I felt that there was a presence in that room. A freezing wind accompanied by the rustling sound passed very close to me. I jumped into bed and wrapped the covers around me, covering my head as well. Then I said the Lord's Prayer several times. I could still hear the rustling.

Now I can almost hear you think, or say, 'Come on, Betsy, that is a burden of lies, a load of rubbish.' But I swear it is the truth. I am not a religious person. I got too confused with so many different theories as to the meaning of the Bible. However I am very God-fearing, and would be afraid to lie, especially about a thing like that. I did not feel unduly afraid, and I was rather tired out, as my son had been born around two o'clock that day. So I slept, in spite of the rustling noise.

I did not mention it to the girl who came in with some breakfast nor to any of the rest. Later another girl came in to dust and polish the floor. I recognised her as one of the girls who had carried me up the stairs after the birth. Yes, believe it or not, the labour room was downstairs and the wards all upstairs. Now I am sure that you can imagine what the stairs inside an old castle look like. Wide, winding, and rather long. The wall going up was hung with portraits.

I had watched the girl's face grow redder, and heard her breathing become difficult. She was at my feet, and another rather stout nurse was at my head, as I lay on a linen stretcher. You can imagine the angle of the stretcher as the poor girl's strength failed. I can see myself going back down that stair quicker than I'm going up it, I thought.

When I told Mother she shook her head saying, 'I've telt ye, lassie, what like they country hantle are. Naebody can put sense into them. You are barely eight stone. What do they do when a woman who weighs sixteen stone comes in? Did ye no' tell them that ye would walk up the stairs?'

'Of course I did, Ma, but they wouldnae heed me. "No, no, no, no," they said. "You have just had a baby. You can't possibly walk up the stairs."'

Mother clicked her tongue, shaking her head again. 'Your Aunt Liza walked hame for three miles after having her wean. Not a soul was wi' her, either. It was a seven-month wean. She just rowed it in her meal-poke then into her shawl and walked hame. She was never any the waur o' it either.'

'Mammy, I'm coming hame wi' ye. When they took my wean in to get fed this morning, I felt his wee feet and they were like icicles. So I put him under the blankets as I fed him. A nurse like Daphne Broon came in and she nearly ate me. "Take that infant out of there at once! That is not hygienic. Out with him!" I was very nearly giving her an answer, but I thought I had better haud my tongue. Anyway, Ma, this place is haunted.'

174

Then I told her about the rustling and the eerie feeling of a presence. 'That would surprise me nane, bairn.' Mother often called us 'bairn'. 'Still, I cannae tak' ye hame the day. The wean would perish wi' the cauld, and maybe yourself tae. I'll go up to Blair the night and try to find somebody wi' a car. I just cannae risk lettin' ye walk hame in this weather. Lexy, run oot and get me a wee bit o' a rowan branch. I noticed rowan trees as we came in.'

Lexy, who had been ben in the nursery, gazing at the baby, had just come in. She did not question Mother's order, but just did as she was asked to, returning not much later with the rowan sprig. She was a bit red-faced. 'You didnae tell me that the woods are hotching wi' soldiers! Englishmen,' she said, 'Grenadier Guards. They thought I was looking for a man. I told them that if I was lookin' for a man that there was little likelihood o' finding one amongst their lot.'

'Oh shaness!' Mother said.

'Well, Ma. You should have heard them,' Lexy answered. 'Real nasty and vulgar they were.'

'Ach dinnae let them get ye bothered, lassie. Here, Betsy, put this ablow your pillow the night.' Mother had put the rowan sprig into a wee paper poke.

She was laughing as she spoke. 'If any o' the nurses find it they will wonder what in the name o' God you are daen wi' it. We will hae tae go now. It will be dark before we get hame. Now remember, bairn. If God be wi' ye naething evil can touch ye.'

Poor Mother was showing signs of the havoc of the war. The uncanny powers of premonition which she possessed were taking their toll of her. Crete had left her almost shattered. Two nephews and two sons of very close friends, all in their early twenties, had perished there. One boy Stewart and one Townsley.

All she wanted to do was work away in the fields. On one or two occasions she went and made herself drunk. She would cry on these occasions and sometimes say, 'Aye, war is a time o' rowans and wild honey, the honey truly sweet and the rowans sairly sour. This is the second war I've seen, and in spite o' aa the sorrow, folk just cannae seem tae see the uselessness o' wars.' Then she would tell us tales of what it was like during the First World War, and after it. 'God gave folk an affie lot, but he was gey sparin' wi' sense,' she often said.

67

My baby son seemed to be all head. His rather thin neck seemed quite unable to support it. Mother put a white silk handkerchief around his neck. This really helped. Wee Mary was delighted with her 'bither' and insisted on pushing him in the pram. She was developing beautifully, in spite of wartime rationing.

Mother tried to teach Katie and me how to understand our weans. How to get to know the reasons for their faults, see their weaknesses and to discipline them by love. If weaknesses were because of lack of mental equipment, then it was useless to push them. 'You cannae put wit whaur there's nane,' was one of Mother's most frequent sayings. 'It's either there, or its no', and nae amount o' schooling or learning will give it to them. So dinnae criticise a wee wean for something that it cannae dae, because it's beyond its power.'

Stories, guessing games, and the singing of rhymes and other songs soon lets one know a lot about children. Their reaction to them is a great guide to the bairn's abilities. Some of Mother's stories, especially those about Silly Jack— a rather simple but kind-hearted and loving character— were meant to lift and cheer the hearts of weans who lacked 'Mother's wit'. Those same stories also helped any child inclined to selfishness or conceit. Silly Jack somehow always succeeded where the arrogant, clever, selfish know-alls had failed.

Mother did not encourage boastfulness, selfishness, nor laziness, and had stories which had this as their theme. She also tried to make us think for ourselves. If we asked a rather stupid question, she would give us a withering look and say, 'Oh, I couldnae tell ye. Go and ask Maggie Clark.' Maggie Clark had been a very well-known simpleton, and the name was used in Mother's family, and still is, in this way. When Mother said 'Ask Maggie Clark' we knew that she meant that the world's greatest simpleton would know the answer to our stupid question.

68

The war continued, but we sort of put our heads into sacks and continued to do productive manual labour on farms, blessing our luck that we were almost living naturally. Of course we watched with mixed emotions the long convoys of laughing soldiers as they drove past. Laughter was their defence—but it had many undertones, visible to the person of understanding, yet full of warmth.

Lots of cousins, friends, and other relatives visited us when home on leave. Quite a few of them had lost the taste for soldiering, and just didn't return to units.

One young friend let his hair grow, and when the police or any other authority came looking for deserters, he would don a skirt and play with a skipping rope, chanting rhymes in a girlish voice. Of course there was a host of skipping girls who had much difficulty suppressing laughter. They were usually only glanced at by the deserter-hunters.

In a row of tents there were sure to be two or three elderly men who played the pipes. Children often spotted the 'ploops', the police, first and at a distance. Then the strains of *Ower the water to Charlie* were played on the pipes, giving warning of their approach. Sometimes escape was impossible. One time three girls bundled their brother under the bed straw and sat on top of him. When the police looked in, only three giggling girls plaiting their hair were to be seen.

The police were sometimes quite ruthless if they caught a

young man suspected of being a deserter, especially if he was of travelling people.

Bryce had a nephew who was unfit for military service. He had nearly lost his life with adhesions after an operation. It was berry-picking time, and John the young lad agreed to take his sisters and me to the pictures in Blairgowrie. We were camped about three miles out. I had no problem about baby-sitters. In an encampment of travellers the children were almost shared.

Anyway, we were just going down the brae towards the bridge in Blair when this police car pulled up alongside of us. Two young policemen jumped out, grabbed young John, twisting his arms up his back. 'Aye, aye, my lad, we've caught you, eh?' Then they threw him head first into the car.

When they drove off, all five of us girls ran after the car, somehow managing to keep it in sight. As we had suspected they did not head for the police station, but to a quiet spot down the water-side. With the added speed and strength of anxiety and fury we weren't long before we reached the car.

There they were: one on each side of John in the back of the car shouting and punching at him. Our fierce love for one another chased any fear of jail or anything else from our minds. 'You bastards!' his oldest sister shouted, lifting a big stone. 'I'll mak' this car into atoms if you don't let him be!' The other three of us were banging on the car windows. Bella certainly would have too—smashed up the car I mean— however the car door opened and they both got out, to be met with what must have seemed like three wildcats.

I helped John out of the car and when I turned round the girls had one policeman on his back and the other was drawing out his baton. 'No you don't!' I shouted and John too rushed at him, grabbing his legs and pulling them from under him. 'Sit on his feet, John!' I shouted, 'and I will see how he likes a taste of the baton!'

'That's a' the good o' ye! Battering a poor wee sick laddie!' I heard Bella shout. 'You would make bonny, brave soldiers. Tak' that! And that!' I heard her thump the policeman's head. Her hands were full of his hair.

I couldn't bring myself to hit the other one. I had just sat down on his face. He still had the freedom of his arms, however, and soon threw me off. Then he picked up his bonnet and shouted to the other one, 'Let them be, Sandy. Come on!'

'Aye, you had better let us be,' I told him, 'but we are not going to let you be. We are going to report you to your superiors. That laddie is just out of hospital, and he is carrying his exempt papers. Furthermore, we are taking him to the nearest doctor.'

John flashed me a look and said, 'Aye, will ye?' This of course meant that in no way would we get him to go to a doctor, but to the policemen, as it would to any non-traveller, it sounded like agreement.

Both policemen looked rather shamefaced now as they dusted themselves down and just stood, looking rather dazed, listening to an avalanche of abuse from John's sisters. Neither of them had a scratch. Traveller girls would not dare to 'mark' a policeman. Neither of them spoke another word, only nodding as they scanned John's papers. Then after handing them back they got into the car and drove away.

'I'm no' hurt,' John insisted, on hearing our anxious enquiries. 'And I'm no' gaun tae any doctor. I've had enough o' doctors.' No amount of persuasion could make him change his mind, although he was the colour of clay.

'When they would do that in the middle o' God's daylight, what would they do on a dark night?' Venom was spitting out of Bella's mouth as she spoke. 'God put a black judgement on them. May they be lying low and tortured in hell before the year is out.' The fate wished on those policemen by the three girls as we headed for home was far worse than any tongue could tell. The words and curses would have sunk a battleship.

However we got a lift on the road from other travellers who were staying at the same berry farm and had an old van. The man got extra petrol coupons to collect scrap metals for re-processing.

Soon John's Mother was flichtering around him anxiously.

179

'I'm a' right, woman. No! I'll no' let you see,' I heard him shout. Meanwhile his father had begun to dismantle the family tents.

Mother asked where they intended going.

'As far awa' as possible,' the woman replied. 'I'll maybe gang ower tae Lumphanan and try tae scrape a living picking cranberries. They should be ready now.'

'We'll miss your company,' Mother said.

'Aye, we will miss yours too, and the girls, but what can a body dae? Once they police tak' a pick at ye they are on your back morning, noon and night. Ready tae pounce on the least pretext.' Then she swore, cursing the police concerned. 'Some o' them young scalpions like tae show off when they get intae a police uniform, and their word is always taken against a traveller.'

We were all near to tears as we watched their laden yoke pull away. Young John was lying back on a comfortable 'bed' in the centre of the float. Normally he would have been walking with the rest.

'Ach, I don't think that I'll bide here either,' Mother declared. 'I think we'll look for a field o' flax somewhere. I never have been aa that fond o' picking berries.'

69

As we waited for the lorry provided by the flax-growers, several women and girls came to say their farewells.

'We'll miss you and the lassies, Maggie,' most of them told her.

'We are gaen tae miss ye aa,' Mother answered, 'but berry-picking was never my cup o' tea.'

'Speaking aboot tea . . .' one woman said, turning to her daughter. 'Run, lassie, and fetch a cup o' tea tae Maggie. Aa her dishes are packed up.'

'I'll come and help you,' I said and added, 'I'll race you!' So we both took off across the field towards her tent. Well,

I have never met a more fitless, han'less, lassie. Twice she fell on the way and upset her mother's milk, spilling every drop. 'Jeannie, for God's sake watch an' no' scald yerself,' I warned her, 'till I run to the farm for milk.'

The farmer's wife told me she had a letter for me. We often used the address of the farm where we worked. I put it in my pocket and hurried back with the milk.

Jeannie was struggling with the tea can. 'Let me,' I told her. 'You carry the cups.' But sure enough she let one fall and break before we got back to our mothers. After dishing out the tea I took out my letter and opened it.

'That man must think an affie lot o' you,' Jeannie remarked. 'You seem tae get letters every ither day.'

I didn't answer her but turned to Mother. 'Ma, he's in hospital!'

She just looked at me. 'It's his back, isn't it? I had some thocht that there was something far wrang wi' it when he couldnae even carry the wean on his last leave.'

'He thinks they are going to discharge him from the Army,' I told her.

'Ach weel, lassie, maybe it's a blessing,' Jeannie's mother put in.

'It *is* his back, Ma. Something to do wi' his spine,' I went on.

'I ken what done that,' Mother said. 'It was that time they were called oot tae lift the rubble off o' folks trapped ablow it.' She could not help adding, 'He was never very hardie, onyway!'

I birsed a bit but said nothing.

'I'll go to the house, Ma, and wait there. The lorry has tae pass through Coupar Angus anyway. I'll ask the driver tae stop and let me off.'

'Aye, you do that, bairn. We'll no' be far awa'. The farm is just the other side o' Burrelton.'

So, taking my two bairns, I went to Mother's house and hastily wrote to Bryce. I could well imagine how lost, uncomfortable and embarrassed he would be feeling. He had never been in hospital before nor had much to do with doctors.

The next few days I spent tidying up Mother's wee bit garden and walking with the weans, drifting into dreams half the time. This has always been my greatest failing. I wake up now and then, scan the world around me and then scuddle back to a world of my own. So most of my life has had a sort of dream-world quality.

Bryce came home in about three weeks' time. He had a letter to give his doctor and his discharge. But would he go to a doctor? Or apply for a pension as was recommended? Not him. 'I'll be all right. I cannae be daen wi' doctors poking aboot wi' me. They'll put me back intae hospital,' he kept saying. 'All right . . . all right,' I told him. 'I'll just let you be.'

Mother and the girls came home to spend a week with us before we left to join his family in Usan. During that week they babied him endlessly—and he lapped it up. It was much the same in Usan with his mother and sisters. I must confess to being guilty too.

70

One day a brother-in-law came in and said, 'Bryce, would you stay here if you had a house?'

Bryce looked at me, I nodded, so Jimmie went on.

'Then there you are. There's a key for you. Gie me thirty shillings and it's yours.'

'Are you leaving, then?' we asked him.

'Aye,' he answered. 'What am I sitting here for? Gazing at a puckle gulls, rocks and water? I'll be in Argyllshire before the week's oot.'

Jimmie had always been an impulsive man. That morning, in a minute, he had decided to move away. We knew that he didn't want the thirty shillings just for the key. They would leave everything, apart from their clothes and bedding, in the house.

I was truly sorry to see them go, as six of their family of

eight were girls. However, like all travelling people, they just had to keep moving. It is only with this sense of freedom that they can get any joy out of living and they are willing to bear discomfort, even hardships, to keep that freedom.

Most people would regard that kind of life as anything but enviable but of course I tend to think there is nothing like it in the world. We have an entirely different way of looking at life. I am not saying it is the right way, but being regarded as the lowest form of humanity can have its advantages! We are free to behave differently—as long as we don't trouble anyone.

Perhaps I should say that we *were* free instead of *are*? And perhaps those days are so sweet to us because they are no more?

Although I felt like Jimmie, I knew that we would have to stay in Usan for a while until I found out how Bryce would manage on the road.

Anyway, Usan was such an open wee village and the few non-travellers who lived there were people used to the country, free and easy to live beside. The bairns could play noisily on the 'street' of hard-baked earth. Nobody shouted at them, except they got into danger, and swans used to waddle up to them to be fed. On warm days it was murder trying to cook over an open grate and the women, travellers and non-travellers, built fires outside.

So having to live there for a wee while in the height of summer was no real hardship. We didn't feel so restricted or hemmed in as we would living in a town.

And I felt content in Jimmie's house. Bryce's sister had polished the black fireplace and it shone, almost twinkled, when I lit the fire to make supper. There were beds a-plenty, a table and chairs, a dresser and a huge wooden kist.

That first night I bathed the weans and Bryce sat with wee Wullie on his knee, playing with him. Little Mary was on my knee, listening to stories—old tales of wonder, magic and strange creatures. Tales which I had learned on my mother's knee and which she had heard in her childhood.

How pleasant, I thought, to have this little place of our own! 'This'll do fine,' I said to Bryce, 'until we get ourselves gathered together. Then maybe we can go off to the country again?'

Glossary

It is doubtful whether the cant, the language of travelling people, is really a language at all—consisting as it does of many words from other languages.

The cant was very useful to travelling people—but only to them. One word could have many meanings and could carry the meaning of a whole sentence, depending on the situation and the tone of voice. In fact, a traveller could appear to be having a normal conversation with a non-traveller—but in reality be giving a message, perhaps a warning, to any traveller listening.

It could be used very cunningly indeed. In wartime it was possible for any intelligent traveller to write home what appeared (even to the best censor) an ordinary simple letter. But it could contain much information to a traveller, such as where the sender was and what was going on around him.

This cunning way of using the cant is dying out rapidly and there is no possible way of retaining it. It is quite impossible to teach to anyone: only by being brought up with it from infancy can it be properly learned. We can *tell* the words to anyone, but *how* to use them is something which will be lost once the travellers of this generation are gone. Even now only about 150 to 200 words remain.

Only a few words are used by young people and children—and those few are almost as familiar to non-travellers, and young people work side by side with non-travellers, some cant words have been integrated too. But most of our young people are so pleased at being accepted, integrated, that they refuse to learn much cant—and even angrily rebuke their parents for using it.

As you will understand, this is a constant source of frustration, disappointment and sadness to the older folk. They see their children and grandchildren—brought up in towns and almost the same as non-travellers—look blankly and stupidly when cant is spoken, not understanding what is being said. And so, sadly, the cant—like the traveller people themselves—is now almost extinct.

Of course we used many ordinary Scots words as well. Most of these I hope you will understand without having to refer to the list on the following pages. There I have tried to explain them all and have included a few notes which I hope you will find interesting. Some of these words we pronounced differently, others had slightly different meanings, from the ways non-travellers used them— but I have shown only *our* way.

a', aa all
abeen above
ablow below
aboot about
aff off
affa awful, terrible; *affie* awfully, terribly
ahint behind
ain own
aince once
airt direction, way
aneath beneath
auld old; *Auld Clootie, Auld Ruchie* the devil; *auld hairy*
   someone who is old and wily for his own ends
awa' away
aweel ah, well!
babbit an eye to shut an eye
bagle a lazy fellow, one who breaks sexual taboos
baith both
bam a fool
bap a bread roll
barming flighty, foolish
barricade This was the central part of a winter tent,
   barricaded from the wind and rain, off which the sleeping
   quarters were built. It was the place for the fire and
   sitting around; the fireplace was in the middle and a hole
   in the roof of the barricade allowed the smoke out

barry   good; *barriest* the best
ben   inside
bicker   to run merrily and noisily
bide   to stay, reside
birse   to bristle, feel annoyed or angry
blether   to talk nonsense, one who does
booie hole   Many inns had a small cubicle no more than a
   metre square, usually near the door. A woman could slip
   in there and order a drink without being seen except by
   the barman. Customers were served through a little hatch
   which could be pushed up
bool-nosed   round-nosed
bothy   a stone hut used as living quarters for unmarried
   farm workers
box   an accordion
braw   fine; *braws* fine clothes
brecham   the collar of a working horse
breest   the breast
brock-basket   a basket for rejected (broken, bruised) fruit
broonie   supposedly a very helpful spirit creature: man-
   shaped, ugly, covered with brown hair, with long feet
   and red eyes. He usually attached himself to a family—
   nearly always millers or farmers—and did the work of
   ten men
brose   a kind of porridge made of uncooked oatmeal, boiling
   water and salted
buckie   a winkle shell
bung   taken, jailed
burker   an intruder. The word originated from William
   Burke who, in the early nineteenth century, murdered
   people to provide corpses for medical research or teaching.
   Travellers were often a target for his activities
burn   a stream
but and ben   a two-room cottage with a room on either
   side of the entrance door
byre   a cowshed
cam   came
cam'   to call

camaschacht clumsy, a stupid person

camp a tent; *camp sticks* tent poles

cannae cannot

canny sensible and safe, moving around carefully, cautious
  ca' canny take care

canter to make mouth music imitating the pipes; *canterach*
  a cantering sound

cauld cold

caw the rope to move your arm as you do when working
  the rope for someone skipping or when you urge a horse
  forward

champ to crush; *champed tatties* mashed potatoes

chap to knock

chirming the singing of birds

chuckie stanes small stone pebbles

claes clothes

claiking clucking, chattering

cleek to walk arm in arm

clocking brooding (hen)

cloots clothes, bedclothes

conyeeched spoiled, petted

cor a stupid person

coronach a Highland dirge, a mournful song

cottar a small house or cottage; one who lives in such a
  dwelling

couldnae couldn't

country hantle the settled, house-dwelling, country people

coup to fall, tumble, overturn

couthy kind, sympathetic

crack to chat, gossip; sociable conversation

cratur creature

cromack a crummock, a walking stick with a curved handle

Cruelty 'A Cruelty' was what we called an Inspector of the
  Royal Society for the Prevention of Cruelty to Children—
  or any official of a local authority.

cutty pipe a short clay pipe

dae to do

daed a lump

dander, daunder a stroll, leisurely walk. 'To go for a dander'
  might also mean to stroll away to relieve oneself
darry a sudden aggressive lunge at someone
daurnae dare not
dee to die
diddle to make mouth music imitating the fiddle
di-does contrary behaviour
dinnae don't
dirty bagle a man who breaks sexual taboos
dirty tail a prostitute
dochter daughter
doldrums in low spirits; weak and confused by drink
doon down
doot to doubt, to think or reckon (depending on the context)
dowie sad
drappie a drop
dreel a drill or row; also a basket
dreich dull, wearisome
drookit drenched, soaked
dunt a thump or knock
dwam a faint or swoon
dyke a stone wall
een eyes
eneuch enough
fa' fall
fae from
faet fault
fairy a child who sees much more than most children do;
  who shows an almost uncanny intuition about things
fang the venomous side of one's nature; *go off the fang* to
  lose one's temper
farm toun a farmstead, a farmhouse, cottages and other
  buildings
fin when
fit what
fitless and han'less footless and handless; apt to stumble,
  clumsy with the hands
flichtering fluttering

floorie   a flower
foo daed . . .?   how do . . .?
forfochen   worn out
forgie   forgive
foundered   collapsed
fower   four
fricht   afraid, fright
fushion   vigour, strength
gadgie   man
gaen, gaun   going
gaered   made to (do something)
gailie   this was something like a *barricade*, which I have
described. A gailie, however, was a bit different in shape:
it was all one height, longer and lower than a barricade
galoot   an idiot, a stupid person
ganch, gansh   to talk too much, to bore someone by talking
in too much detail
gang   to go, travel
garron   a strong horse you could depend on, even though
it might be of inferior breed
gaswork cinders   coke
gaun   going
gear   possessions
gey   very
gie   to give; *gie us a crack* give (me) some conversation, let's
have a chat; *gie him his tatties* give him what he deserves
gin   if
glaikit   silly, senseless
glaur   mud, ooze
gled   glad
glisk   a sparkle
gloaming   dusk, twilight
go off the fang   to lose one's temper
gogged eggs   half-hatched eggs
graip   a pitchfork
granny sooker   a pan drop, a peppermint sweet
greet   to weep; *grat* wept
grumfie   a pig

grund the ground
guffie a boorish, unfeeling, cruel person
gulder a loud angry shout
gutters muddy puddles
hae to have
haet a small piece, a morsel
hailie-wracket muddle-headed, yet daring to try or say
  anything
hairst harvest
hap to dress a child; to tuck up in bed
hardie strong, robust
haud to hold
haver to talk nonsense
hert a heart; *hert of corn* the salt of the earth, none
  better
hoo how
hooch the shout given during the dancing of the reel
hornies the police
how-an-ever however
howlet an owl
huke a sickle
hurl a lift on the road
in-aboot in-about: a traveller expression which cannot be
  translated by 'come in' because you do not come *in* to an
  encampment as you come in to a house. You come within
  the general area of tents, fire, parked carts and tethered
  ponies. You come in-aboot from any direction and may
  move about greeting people at their various occupations
  in different parts of the encampment
inbye nearer
ither other
jeely-jar jam-jar
jill a gill
John Barleycorn whisky
jugal a dog
kist a box or chest for storage
knowe a small hill
laich low

lee-lang whole
lee-leaf-alane quite alone
limmer a rascal or rogue; a loose girl
loon a lad
loo-ral a shout (The sound 'loo-ral' carries a long way)
loup to jump, leap; *loup a laich dyke* to jump over a
  low wall
lowsing time unyoking (loosening) time, time to stop work
lug an ear
mairt, mart a market
mannies men
marrow a partner, equal; *marrowless* odd, without a
  partner
maun must; *maun dae is a guid maister* 'must do' is a
  good master
meal poke a meal bag, a bag for food
meek a quiet sound made by an infant or by a pet, to
  mew or whine
midden a rubbish heap or dung heap; a term of abuse,
  particularly to a woman
min man
mind, mind on to remember
miscaa' to miscall, to scold, to call names
moich foolish, mad
mony many
moo mouth
moose a house
mootyay a rabbit
muskin a mutchkin, a measure of liquid
na, nae no
nakens travellers
nane none
nash avree! get moving!
neeps turnips; *neep-tasted* tasting of turnips
nicker to whinny
o' of
ower over
oxter armpit

pea-alleys the game of hop-scotch
pech, peek to pant for breath
peeked-looking sickly-looking
pickle, puckle a small quantity, a few
plank! hide!
ploo a plough
ploops the police
plouter to potter about on trifling tasks
pluchie a ploughman
plukie-faced pimple-faced
plunk to pluck out
polis the police
prig to plead
puckle a small quantity, a few
puddock a frog
quean, queen, quine a girl
raise the wind to earn enough to survive
ranny a bold unruly person
rax to stretch, overstrain
reed a cattle pen
reel-rall helter-skelter
rin to run
ripe, rype to search
rive to tear apart, to eat ravenously
roon round
rowed wrapped up
rummle to shake
sair, sairly sore, sorely
sateen a linen or cotton cloth woven in such a way that it
   has a gloss like satin
sax six
scaffy, sciffy a maidservant, also a refuse collector
scald to cause grief or pain
scaldified behaving like scaldies, town-dwellers of the lowest
   class. (*Scaldie* originally meant 'bare': bare of feet, money,
   clothes)
scalpions roguish young men, eager to work off high spirits
   by tormenting others

scarify to scrub all over very roughly

sconce to tease, especially in a way which belittles the person

scoor, scoorin' to scatter, scattering

scouff, scouth freedom, sufficient space to romp and play

scranny thin, wizened

scrunted a scrunted tree is one that is still standing but is decayed inside and covered with moss and lichens

scud to smack, a smack

scuddle to scurry or hasten, particularly in order to avoid work or responsibilities

shaness! an exclamation meaning 'bad word', 'bad deed' or 'bad situation' but it can be used in many different ways

share sure

shern cow dung

shuch the private part of a woman

siller silver

skirlie seasoned fried oatmeal

skirling shrill screaming

sleekit sly, cunning

smeeked smelling of, and cheery with, drink

sneck a latch

snooled made to feel low and downtrodden

soo a heap of loose hay or straw

soaken to soak

sook to suck

souch, sough a murmur: of the sea, a river, the wind, distant voices, birds' wings, for example

spall, spawl to spald, tear apart

speekit a spigot, a tap. Actually a speekit was a small hole in a barrel with a stopper. Often country people had to use water from a barrel which had a tap to turn on the water, so in course of time a tap came to be known as a speekit

spey-wife a woman fortune-teller

spin-drift fierce hail or snow which seems to come from all directions

spit a likeness

stall to stop, keep one's self-control

stane a stone

stirr to get someone excited, all worked up

stovies sliced potatoes steamed with fried onions

stooks sheaves of grain set up against each other to dry

swey a fire iron. It hung above the fire and had a hinge which allowed it to be swung forward to remove a pot or kettle. It could then be swung back over the fire or to the side if not needed

syne since

tail a loose woman

tak' to take; *tak' tent* take notice

tap to top, to cut the tops off turnips or sugar beet. The tool used was called a *tapner*

tappie a decoration made of straw for the top of grain stacks

tatties potatoes

telt told

thocht thought

thon that one

thrang crowded, close together

thrawn obstinate

til to

toich a smell

troosh to humble or frighten someone

troot a trout

tuggery fine clothes

twa two

umman body a woman

waa' a wall

wad would

walsh dried up and bad-tasting

wassle to wrestle

watter water

waur worse

wean a child

wee little, small

weel well

wha, whae who
whammle to turn upside down
whaur where, why? for what reason?
wheeple to whistle
wheesht! hush! be quiet!
whin the gorse bush
whittle a knife similar to a butcher's chopper; to cut away
   in woodcarving
wi' with
wid would
winna, winnae will not
wonner wonder
wordie a word
wrang wrong
wye way
yin one
yirdy a toad
yoke a pony and cart (that is, the two yoked together); to
   attach a pony to a cart
yon yonder, that one
yowe a ewe